CREATE YOUR
REALITY
JOURNAL

Breakthrough Limiting Patterns:
7 Life-Changing Habits to Cultivate
a Mindset of "I Can and I Will".

BY PREETIE BOLER

This Journal belongs to

If found, please contact:

The tool to design your reality

The simplest, most effective way to shift from limiting
patterns to a mindset that unlocks your full potential.

Viktor Frankl's Freedom to Choose

*Between a thought or emotion and an action or reaction there is a
space. Within this space is a pause... and in this pause we are allowed to
choose. And it's within this choice lies our growth and freedom.*

Choose what serves you.

Choose what aligns to your vision and values.

Choose to honour the five-year-old and eighty-year-old within you.

Created by:
Preetie Boler

Published by:
Empowered by Design

For more information or to be a Stockist, please contact: Info@empoweredbydesign.com.au

ISBN: 978-0-646-89190-3

Be in pursuit of your full potential – success and happiness will follow

Preetie Boler

There is magic within you. Only you can access this magic.

Once unlocked, you can create the reality your heart desires.

This journal will be your personal mentor for the next three months.

YOU ARE READY!

Contents

.

A Message from The Author

It was September 18th, 2006, a day clearly etched in my memory. I found myself lying on the cold tiles of my bathroom floor, facing the crossroads of my life. I was in a place of profound despair. I was grappling with an intense, endless battle of self-doubt and feelings of 'not good enough'. My marriage had died a slow death. My only child loved his nanny more than me, his mother. I'd let my dad down. I was grappling with feeling like a failure as a wife, a failure as a mother, and a failure as a daughter. Each day felt like an insurmountable struggle, and, despite professional help, I found myself lost in a haze of prescriptive drugs. I was ready to escape from my pain and suffering and end it all.

After six hours on that bathroom floor, as if guided by an unforeseen force, I stood up and walked determinedly to my desk. There, I began to write, to pour my heart out onto a notepad. Words flowed, unrestrained, unfiltered—every ounce of my pain, guilt, shame, fears, hopes, and dreams were transferred to paper. Eighteen pages later, I had before me a commitment to myself.

Those eighteen pages were the seeds of my transformation. That outpouring from my soul was the essence of what I now call the R.E.A.L.I.T.Y. Blueprint—the seven elements that became the pillars for rebuilding my life. That journal didn't just help me, it saved me. It was the tool that enabled me to awaken my inner strength, confront my demons, unlock my full potential, and chart a new reality for my future. A reality that I am so very proud of today.

The adoption of the R.E.A.L.I.T.Y. Blueprint marked a monumental shift in my mindset and consequently, in my life. Each of the seven elements acted like a compass point, guiding me through the fog of despair towards a life of clarity, purpose, and fulfilment. Embracing Responsibility taught me the power of taking charge of my life, owning my choices and their outcomes, transforming me from being a passive onlooker to an active participant in my life's narrative. Engaging with each element—Embracing Change, Authentic Living, Love, Innovation, Time, and Honouring 'You'—was like turning a key, unlocking potential within me I hadn't realised existed.

As I practised these principles, I noticed profound changes. Challenges became opportunities for growth, not obstacles. Authenticity brought a sense of peace and alignment, replacing the turmoil of pretending, trying to fit in and living someone else's life. Love and compassion, directed inward and outward, healed old wounds, and fostered meaningful connections. Innovation and continuous learning fuelled my curiosity and passion, driving personal and professional advancement. Living in the present allowed me to appreciate the now, reducing anxieties tied to past experiences and future worries. Most importantly, learning to honour and respect myself laid the foundation for a life built on self-worth and confidence.

This holistic transformation was not an overnight occurrence for me but a journey of small, consistent steps, each guided by the blueprint. It was a metamorphosis from a place of pain to a life rich with purpose and joy. The R.E.A.L.I.T.Y. Blueprint was more than just a framework; it was the catalyst that propelled me from the depths of despair to heights I had never imagined possible.

Now, imagine if you could break through barriers, let go of limiting patterns, unlock your full potential, and rise to new heights, all while staying true to yourself and nurturing your own heart. Imagine a world where you take charge of your destiny, where challenges become stepping stones to success, and where self-doubt is replaced with unshakable confidence. The seven core principles of the blueprint will be your GPS on this journey. They will be the default mechanism for shifting your mindset to elements that will serve you, that will awaken your true potential.

Sharing this blueprint within a journal isn't just about imparting knowledge, it's about giving you the gift of the transformative power of journaling. It's not just a diary, it's your daily companion on the path to a positive mindset, letting go of limiting patterns, self-discovery, resilience, and boundless achievement. Think of it as a sanctuary for your thoughts, a canvas for your dreams, and a blueprint for your growth.

With each stroke of your pen, you'll embrace personal responsibility, conquer change, and become the authentic, innovative, and compassionate force that the world needs. You'll learn to dance gracefully between the past and future, anchored in the richness of the present moment. And you'll come to honour and respect the remarkable person you see in the mirror, embracing self-acceptance as your superpower.

This journal is not just pages; it's a promise to yourself. It's a commitment to becoming the unstoppable force you were always meant to be. It's an invitation to rise, shine, and conquer the world on your terms.

Are you ready to rise to the moment? The journey begins with your pen, your thoughts, and your heart.

With this journal let's embark on this incredible journey of creating your new reality through cultivating the 7 life-changing habits for a growth mindset.

With an unwavering belief in your potential,

Preetie Boler

Instructions for Using the Journal

1. **Identify Your Limiting Barriers**

   Begin by recognising and understanding the personal barriers that hold you back from growth and progression in life.

2. **Set Your Intentions**

   Then set clear intentions for using the journal. What specific goals or areas of personal and professional development do you want to focus on? Write these intentions down in the prepared pages of the journal.

3. **Daily Prompts and Reflections**

   Start each day by reflecting on one of the seven core principles, rotating through them on a weekly basis.

   Read the daily prompt related to the principle and take a moment to consider how it applies to your life and work. Then, at the end of the day, reflect on how the day unfolded for you.

4. **Journal Your Thoughts**

   Write down your thoughts, experiences, and actions related to the daily principle. Be honest and open in your reflections. Use the journal as a safe space to explore your feelings and insights.

   Journalling about what you're grateful for transforms your lens on life. It can help focus on your blessings and deepen your appreciation for the everyday miracles.

5. **Set a Plan for Actions**

   After your daily reflection, consider setting a plan for actions related to the principle. Think about how you can implement the principle in your daily life and career.

6. **Track Your Progress**

   Use the journal to track your progress. Document your achievements, setbacks, and lessons learned. Regularly revisit your goals and actions to assess your growth.

7. **Weekly Check-Ins**

   At the end of each week, use the provided notes pages to conduct a weekly check-in. Reflect on your overall progress, what went well, and what challenges you faced. Adjust your goals if necessary.

8. **Inspirational Content**

   Pay attention to the inspirational quotes and affirmations throughout the journal. Use them as motivation and reminders of your commitment to growth. They are your identity affirmations and worldview affirmations.

9. **Celebrate Your Achievements**

   Celebrate your successes, both big and small. Acknowledge your progress and the positive changes you've made in your life and career.

10. **Long-Term Commitment**

    Remember that the journal is not a one-time activity or a New Year's resolution. It's a lifelong commitment to your personal and professional growth. Embrace the journey, and trust that consistent practice of these core principles will lead to lasting transformation.

11. **Become the Master and Leader of Your Reality**

    Use this journal as a powerful tool for shifting your mindset towards self-discovery, professional and personal growth, empowerment, and leadership.

Choices   Clarity   Commitment   Consistency   Celebrations

Start with making a '**choice**' on what you want and who you want to become. Have '**clarity**' on your goals and the vision of the reality you desire. '**Commit**' to the process, and over time with '**consistency**', you will witness positive changes in your career and life as you shift from feeling stagnated to becoming the master and leader of your own destiny. Don't forget to '**celebrate**' your accomplishments. These Five Cs will be the thread that will be woven through this transformation journey.

Your Reality is an
Echo of Your Beliefs
and Behaviours

The Transformative Power of Journaling

You might be wondering how the simple act of writing in a journal can help you achieve your goals and design a reality you desire.

Well, this journal is not just about jotting down random thoughts. It's about consciously committing your goals, dreams, and aspirations to paper, and taking action guided by a framework. This act of writing down your goals is like signing a contract with yourself.

Journaling serves as an incredibly powerful visualisation tool enabling you to vividly paint the reality you desire. It also aids in deep self-reflection, allowing you to identify key areas for improvement, it allows you to meticulously track your progress and celebrate your achievements.

The practice of journaling has also been linked to increased self-awareness and self-reflection, fostering personal growth and emotional resilience. Numerous experts and research studies have validated the benefits of journaling. It's been recognised not just as a tool for emotional expression, but also as a beneficial practice for mental and physical health.

According to a study by Dr. James Pennebaker of the University of Texas, Austin, expressive writing, a form of journaling, can lead to improved mental and physical health. Research by psychologists Laura King and Joshua Smyth found that expressive writing can lead to reductions in stress and anxiety, improvements in mood, and even better cognitive functioning.

When we pour our deepest thoughts and desires onto paper, we're not just crafting words; we're setting intentions, inspiring and motivating as well as healing. Our minds find solace, our hearts find peace, and our bodies respond with a newfound lightness.

As you embrace this practice, you will find yourselves on a journey of self-discovery and growth, each page a stepping stone to self-awareness, authenticity, resilience, and joy. So, as you journey through these pages, remember they are more than just a space for words; they are a canvas for unlocking your true potential to achieve success, happiness, and fulfilment.

Journaling played a pivotal role in my transformation, allowing me to untangle complex emotions and thoughts and translate them into clear, actionable insights. The daily practice of reflection became more than just a habit; it was my trusted companion and confidante, guiding me from a state of despair and confusion to a newfound depth of self-understanding and a life filled with purpose and clarity.

The 7 Reasons this Journal is Critical for You

1. **Self-awareness**

    Journaling helps you become more self-aware by encouraging regular reflection on your thoughts, behaviours, and actions in alignment with each core principle. It allows you to gain insight into your strengths and areas for improvement.

2. **Goal Setting and Tracking**

    By journaling about how you apply each core principle daily, you can set clear goals and track your progress over time. This process promotes accountability and motivation to consistently practice these principles.

3. **Stress Reduction**

    The act of journaling, particularly in relation to the core principle of "Living in the Present Moment," can help alleviate stress and anxiety. It provides a space to unload worries and refocus on the present, fostering a sense of calm.

4. **Personal & Professional Growth**

    Journaling your experiences with the seven core principles can contribute to your personal and professional development. As you record your actions and reflections, you can identify strategies that lead to success and make adjustments where needed.

5. **Enhanced Problem-Solving**

    Journaling encourages innovative thinking and problem-solving, aligning with the core principle of "Being in an Innovative Mode." It allows you to brainstorm and explore creative solutions to challenges you encounter.

6. **Positive Mindset**

    Regularly reflecting on your efforts to practice self-compassion, empathy, and other principles under "Holding Space for Love in Your Heart" can cultivate a more positive and compassionate mindset. It helps you develop a kinder attitude toward yourself and others.

7. **Greater Resilience**

    As you journal about embracing change and challenges, you build resilience and adaptability. Over time, this practice can help you become more resilient in the face of adversity and more open to growth opportunities.

I was caught up in a whirlwind of despair and confusion, and it felt like I was just stuck there. Journaling became this critical tool for me, not just to vent, but to really make sense of all that chaos in my head. It's like it gave me a ladder to climb out of that mess and start seeing things clearer, finding my way to a life that actually feels purposeful and right. That's why journaling has been so huge for me."

Common Personal Barriers and Their Impact on Our Lives

Have you found yourself standing at the edge of success, at the edge of something good... something that's going to put you on the path of your best future ... only to feel an invisible force pulling you back, sabotaging your progress?

Perhaps, it was that inner voice telling you that you're not good enough, not smart enough, or deserving enough. The voice that says, why bother... you are going to fail anyway.

Do you sometimes feel you are your own worst enemy?

That is the limiting patterns that plays-up for us as a result of our habitual beliefs, thoughts, and behaviours. These patterns are manifestation of self-sabotage. If allowed to control our lives, will hold us back from professional and personal growth and progression.

12 Common Personal Barriers and their Impact on Professional Development.

1. Self-Doubt

    Self-doubting statements such as, I'm not good enough, I don't deserve it, and I'm just born unlucky can fill our minds.

    Self-doubt often manifests as a persistent feeling of uncertainty about one's abilities, talents, or accomplishments. Questioning one's abilities or worthiness for a role or task can lead to missed opportunities, as we may hesitate to apply for promotions or take on new challenges.

2. Lack of Confidence

    A lack of confidence can limit the willingness to seek promotions, negotiate salaries, or take on leadership roles. It may also hinder us from voicing opinions or contributing ideas, leading to missed opportunities for recognition and growth.

3. Resistance to Change

    Being resistant to change can for example, make it difficult to adapt in dynamic work environments. This resistance can result in missed opportunities for learning new skills or taking on different responsibilities that could lead to career advancement.

4. Fear of Challenges

    A fear of facing challenges can prevent us from stepping out of our comfort zones, and even limit our personal and professional development. This fear might stop us from tackling complex projects or innovative initiatives that require risk-taking and problem-solving.

5. **Inauthenticity**

   Inauthenticity, or not being true to oneself, can lead to dissatisfaction and burnout. It can create a gap between personal vision, values and professional life, resulting in decreased motivation and engagement at work.

6. **Imposter Syndrome**

   This syndrome, where one feels undeserving of their achievements, can result in constant self-doubt and anxiety. It might hinder us from accepting high-profile projects or promotions due to fear of being 'exposed' as a fraud.

7. **Lack of Empathy**

   In leadership roles, a lack of empathy can affect team cohesion and morale. It can hinder the development of strong, trust-based relationships with colleagues, which are essential for collaborative work environments.

8. **Lack of Self-Compassion**

   Being overly critical of oneself can lead to heightened stress and decreased resilience. This lack of self-compassion can make it challenging to bounce back from setbacks or to balance personal and professional responsibilities effectively.

9. **Lack of Self-Acceptance**

   Struggling with self-acceptance can lead to a constant pursuit of external validation. This can result in a lack of intrinsic motivation and fulfilment as achievements are overshadowed by an ongoing sense of inadequacy.

10. **People-pleasing tendencies**

    Prioritising others' needs and opinions over one's own, and constantly trying to please others can lead to burnout and resentment. It might also result in neglecting one's own needs and goals, limiting personal growth and professional advancement.

11. **Ruminating on Past Mistakes**

    Dwelling on past errors can lead to a fear of failure, stifling creativity and innovation. This focus on past mistakes can prevent learning from experiences and moving forward constructively.

12. **Perfectionism**

    Needing to be perfect. We may feel pressured to meet extremely high standards, leading to an excessive focus on perfection. This can hinder progress as we may hesitate to take risks or make decisions for fear of making mistakes.

There was a time in my life when barriers seemed like towering walls, impossible to climb. My biggest barrier was that 'I was a failure'. My mind was clouded with doubts – 'What if I fail... again? What if they judge me?' At a personal level, the fear was so intense that I remained in a marriage for 4 years after its demise as I feared I would fail as a single mum. I feared I would let people down. I feared the stigma... 'a divorcee'. Something my culture and community frowned upon.

At a professional level, because of my people-pleasing tendencies, I feared I would offend others if I spoke up or asserted myself. I was also afraid of feedback and would immediately judge myself as being not good enough.

I've learned, barriers are often the guardians of our greatest potentials, waiting to be challenged. Overcoming them doesn't just change what we do; it changes who we are, who we become. And that's what I hope for you – to see your barriers as steppingstones, leading you to the heights of your own untapped potential.

From the list of Twelve Common Barriers here, what are your top three barriers?

And how has each of these barriers held you back?

1.

2.

3.

Self-Sabotage

If we fail to break through our personal barriers, limiting patterns and instead we allow them to take charge, and run our lives, it can manifest as self-sabotage.

Self-sabotage has been defined as the deliberate or unconscious behaviours, thoughts, emotions, beliefs or actions that hinder an individual's progress or success, often undermining their own goals, well-being, or happiness.

Self-sabotage keeps us in a fixed mindset or victim mindset. And its main objective is to hold us back from reaching our full potential, and our best life.

Here's a list of self-sabotaging behaviours that showcase a victim mindset:

1. **External Blame**

   Attributing challenges and failures to external circumstances or other people, rather than recognizing one's own role or ability to influence the situation. 'It's not my fault; they made me do it.' 'It's because of you my life is this way.' 'It's my mother's fault'.

2. **Feeling Powerless**

   Believing that there's nothing one can do to change or improve their circumstances. 'Things will never get better for me, or I'm just born unlucky.'

3. **Catastrophic Thinking**

   Always expecting the worst-case scenario or exaggerating the negativity of a situation. 'Every time I try, something bad always happens.'

4. **Resenting Others' Success**

   Believing others have it easier and harbouring resentment towards them for it. 'Of course, they succeeded; they've always had everything handed to them.'

5. **Resistance to Help or Solutions**

   When presented with potential solutions or assistance, focus on why they won't work rather than considering their merits. 'That might work for others, but not for me.'

6. **Constant Complaining**

   Often talking about problems but not taking steps to address them. 'My life is just miserable, and it's always going to be this way. Nothing good ever happens to me.'

7. **Rejection of Personal Responsibility**

   Avoiding accountability and often feeling attacked when one's actions or decisions are pointed out. 'It's not my fault; the team always lets me down, and the workload is impossible to manage.'

8. **Belief in Unfairness**

   Thinking the world is inherently against them. 'Why do bad things always happen to me?'

Here's a list of self-sabotaging behaviours that demonstrate a fixed mindset:

1. **Avoidance of Challenges**

   Believing that if something is hard it's not meant for you. Avoiding tasks because they feel difficult or outside one's comfort zone. 'If it's this hard, it's probably not something I'm supposed to do. I'll stick to what I know I can handle easily.'

2. **Fear of Change / Fear of Failure**

   Holding back or not trying at all due to the fear that failure would confirm a lack of ability or intelligence. 'If I don't get the job, it'll just prove I'm not as smart or capable as others think I am.'

3. **Intelligence is Static**

   Believing that you're born with a certain level of intelligence and there's nothing you can do to change it. Making statements like, 'I'm just not good at math.'

4. **Feedback as a Threat**

   Taking constructive criticism personally or seeing it as an attack, rather than an opportunity for improvement. 'My boss is always finding fault in my work; she must think I'm incompetent.'

5. **Feeling Threatened by Others' Success**

   Instead of being inspired or learning from the success of peers, feeling insecure or envious. 'Every time someone else succeeds, it just highlights my failures and inadequacies.

6. **Attributing Success to External Factors**

   Believing that achievements are due to luck or external factors rather than one's own effort or abilities. 'I just got lucky.'

7. **Stagnation**

   Sticking to what's familiar or easy, rather than pushing oneself to learn and grow. 'Why bother with all that extra effort? I'm fine with where I am and what I know.'

8. **Belief in Predestined Fate**

   Thinking that the future is set in stone and no amount of effort can change one's path or outcomes. 'Why bother with all that extra effort? I'm fine with where I am and what I know.'

9. **Avoidance of Feedback**

   Actively avoiding opportunities for feedback or review because of the fear of negative comments. 'If I don't hear it, then I won't have to deal with potential negative feedback, which is just too stressful.'

10. **Defensiveness**

    When challenged or given feedback, responding with defensiveness and excuses rather than openness to learn. 'You don't understand the challenges I faced. My approach was the only reasonable one under the circumstances.'

Self-sabotage is a universal challenge that many face in various forms.

Which of the above self-sabotaging behaviours do you struggle with the most?

Do you have a victim or fixed mindset?

In my past, I often convinced myself that I wasn't good enough or that failure was inevitable. This cycle of self-sabotage became like a comfort zone for me, my excuse not to take action, a familiar yet destructive space to be in.

The Disempowering Cycle of Self-Sabotage

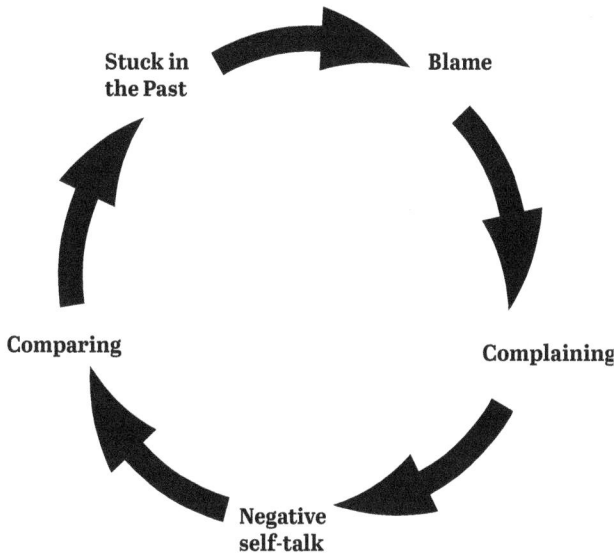

Stuck in the Past

Blame

Comparing

Complaining

Negative self-talk

CAUSES NEGATIVE
VIBRATIONS
THAT PROMOTE:

Lack

Less

Small

Scarcity

Fear

Hardship

Difficult

Unpleasant

How do these elements impact us and our lives?

1. Hindered personal growth and well-being:

    Being stuck in the past and engaging in negative self-talk often leads to a lack of self-esteem and self-worth. This mindset traps you in a cycle of regret, guilt, shame and missed opportunities, preventing personal growth, and negatively affecting mental health.

2. Damaged relationships and social interactions:

    Habitual blaming and constant complaining can strain personal and professional relationships. These behaviours create a negative atmosphere that can repel others, leading to isolation and difficulties in maintaining healthy relationships. Engaging in destructive patterns can undermine trust and intimacy.

3. Reduced professional effectiveness and opportunities:

    In a professional setting, negative self-talk, and a habit of comparing oneself with others can significantly diminish confidence and performance. This mindset often manifests as an unconscious desire to stay in a comfort zone, resulting in missed opportunities for advancement and can hamper one's ability to collaborate effectively with colleagues.

4. It causes impaired decision-making:

    Self-sabotage can also cloud judgment and impair decision-making abilities. This can lead to making poor choices, impulsive actions, or a reluctance to take calculated risks, ultimately hindering professional growth and success.

How has self-sabotage impacted your life? (Be completely honest and free with your response here)

Clinging to self-sabotage is like holding the anchor that drowns us, yet the strength to release it lies within us, unlocking the currents of potential that propel us towards our true destiny.

Reflecting on Your Limiting Patterns

These questions help you with introspection and self-evaluation to better understand and identify your personal barriers to growth. To recognise the mindset that holds you back.

Please answer these questions honestly and reflectively for greater self-awareness and self-discovery.

Self-Awareness

What are the recurring negative thoughts or emotions I often experience?

How do they impact my decisions and actions?

Limiting Beliefs

What beliefs do I hold about myself that might be limiting my growth or happiness?

Where do these beliefs come from? Are they true?

Fear and Avoidance ————————————————————————

What am I most afraid of in terms of personal growth or success?

What opportunities have I avoided due to fear?

Reaction to Criticism ————————————————————————

How do I typically react to criticism or feedback?

Do I find myself getting defensive or dismissive, and why might that be?

Comparison with Others ————————————————

Do I often compare myself to others?

How does this comparison make me feel about my own achievements and capabilities?

Comfort Zone ————————————————

What aspects of my life or work am I staying in because it's comfortable, even though it doesn't fulfill me?

What is stopping me from pursuing something that's more fulfilling?

Responsibility and Blame

In challenging situations, do I tend to take responsibility, or do I find myself placing blame on others or external circumstances?

Facing Challenges ————————————————————————

When faced with a difficult situation, what is my initial response?

Do I confront it, seek solutions, or tend to shy away from it?

Perception of Failure ————————————————————————

How do I view failure?

Do I see it as a learning opportunity or as a defining aspect of my identity?

Emotional Expression

Do I feel comfortable expressing my emotions, both positive and negative?

If not, what holds me back?

Change and Adaptability

How do I feel about change?

Am I open to it, or do I resist it, and what are the reasons for my attitude towards change?

Acknowledging Success

How do I react to my successes?

Do I acknowledge and celebrate them, or do I downplay or dismiss them?

Self-Care and Self-Compassion

How do I practice self-care and self-compassion?

Do I prioritize my well-being or tend to neglect it?

Seeking Help or Support ———————————————————

Am I comfortable seeking help or support when needed?

What barriers prevent me from reaching out?

Long-Term Goals and Visions ———————————————————

What are my long-term goals and visions for myself?

What might be stopping me from pursuing them?

Self-discovery is a journey that winds through the depths of our being, revealing not just who we are, but who we have the potential to become.

You Are Capable of The Shift

You can shift your mindset to a version of yourself that is thriving, healthy, happy, abundant, and pleasant.

1. Did you know that your thoughts, beliefs, and behaviour patterns have a powerful impact on shaping your reality? It's true. Your thoughts can either hold you back or propel you forward towards the life you desire.

2. Have you ever heard of the term neuroplasticity? It's a fascinating concept based on scientific research that explains how the brain has a truly remarkable ability to rewire itself forming brand-new neural pathways in response to our thoughts, experiences, and behaviours. Simply put, by consciously and purposefully directing our thoughts in a positive, optimistic and constructive direction, we can literally reshape our brain and, in turn, our reality. *(Becoming Supernatural by Dr. Joe Dispenza).*

3. Remember your mind is like a garden and your thoughts are the seeds. You have the choice of growing weeds or flowers. When you plant seeds of positivity and empowering beliefs, when you nurture them with affirmations and align them with actions, you'll reap a bountiful harvest of success and fulfilment. *(Think and Grow Rich by Napolean Hill).*

4. By recognising the limiting factors and shifting your mindset against these barriers, especially by using the seven core practices in this journal as a default mechanism, we can transform their limiting beliefs, self-doubt and inner negative narratives and unlock their true potential, leading to a more fulfilling and successful reality.

5. We have a choice to either allow life to happen to us, where we are mere passengers on this journey or to become the masterful drivers steering our course towards all that we desire. It's about making the conscious choice to cultivate a mindset and belief that 'I am the leader and master of my professional and personal life'.

When I found myself at a crossroads of life, I felt stuck in a pattern of negativity and self-doubt. It was like being in a loop of constant setbacks, and my mindset at the time – a fixed one – only saw these as confirmations of my limitations.

Through self-discovery, I realised, my mindset, not my capabilities, that was the real barrier. That was my turning point. I began to practice mindset shifts… embracing the belief that I can turn my life around. That power was within me.

This shift didn't happen overnight. It required conscious effort. I practiced self-awareness and started journaling, setting small, achievable goals, committing to the plan, and facing challenges as an opportunity to learn and grow.

Today, I look back and realise that adopting a growth mindset was the catalyst for a complete life transformation. Leaving my marriage, moving countries, getting requalified as a lawyer in Australia, being a proud mum, leading a successful team at work, fearlessly putting my hand up for every opportunity for growth and progression. This journey has taught me that the true power to change my life always lay within my own mindset.

Mindset shift: where the mind's weeds of doubt are uprooted, making space for the blossoming flowers of possibility and growth.

A Growth Mindset

The concept of 'growth mindset' as defined by *Dr Carol S Dweck (Author of Mindset)* is a belief that our abilities and intelligence can be developed through dedication and hard work. It's all about changing the way you think; changing your mindset to unlock your full potential.

People with a growth mindset believe that their abilities can be developed with effort, learning, and perseverance. They see challenges and failures as opportunities to learn and grow.

Our mindset shapes our behaviour, attitude towards challenges, and resilience in the face of setbacks.

The Five Core Benefits of a Growth Mindset

1. **Enhanced Learning and Adaptability**

    Individuals with a growth mindset are more open to learning from experiences. They view challenges and unfamiliar situations as opportunities to learn and grow, making them more adaptable to change.

2. **Resilience in the Face of Setbacks**

    Those with a growth mindset are less likely to give up when they encounter obstacles. Instead of viewing setbacks as failures, they see them as feedback and an integral part of the learning process. This resilience often leads to long-term achievement.

3. **Increased Motivation**

    A growth mindset fosters intrinsic motivation. People become more driven by the intrinsic joy of learning and growing rather than external rewards or approval. This intrinsic motivation can lead to greater persistence and effort in pursuits.

4. **Better Relationships and Collaboration**

    Those with a growth mindset are generally more receptive to feedback, leading to more constructive communication. They're less likely to feel threatened by others' success and are more likely to celebrate it, fostering positive relationships and more effective collaboration.

5. **Continuous Personal and Professional Development**

    Individuals with a growth mindset are proactive in seeking opportunities to develop new skills and expand their knowledge base. They remain lifelong learners, always looking for ways to improve and evolve, which can lead to personal satisfaction and professional advancement.

Having a growth mindset isn't just a skill, it's a tool to thrive. It removes ceilings from our potential, and we view challenges and obstacles as stepping stones, not stumbling blocks.

You're in charge of your mind. You can help it grow by using it in the right way.

With Dr Carol Dweck's definition of a growth mindset–A belief that abilities and intelligence can be developed through dedication and hard work–in mind, think about the following questions.

How do you develop this belief?

What thoughts do you need to have?

What emotions do you need to feel?

What behaviour patterns do you need to demonstrate?

What habits do you need to cultivate?

Read on.

The R.E.A.L.I.T.Y Blueprint - The Seven Core Principles to Cultivate a Growth Mindset

The R.E.A.L.I.T.Y. Blueprint

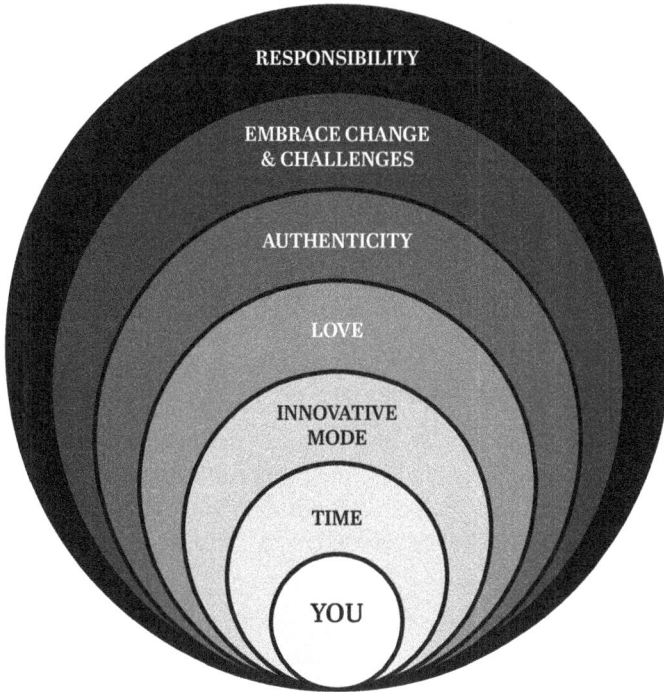

The R.E.A.L.I.T.Y Blueprint is designed as a simple, practical and accessible guide for shifting from a fixed or victim mindset to one that unlocks your true potential. These seven core principles lay the groundwork for cultivating habits that promote a growth mindset

By mastering each principle and creating habits around these elements, you gradually transform your life from a state of feeling stuck and victimized to becoming the master and leader of your own journey. This blueprint is more than just a set of practices; it's a transformative tool that mirrors your relationship with yourself and the world.

It's been said, reality is a mirror that reflects your relationship with yourself and the world around you. If you want to become a true creator of your magnificent reality, you need to embody these empowering practices. Trust me. These practices are the key to your full potential.

The R.E.A.L.I.T.Y. Blueprint and how they relate to personal and professional growth.

1. Responsibility

    Choose personal responsibility over blame. Blaming others and playing the victim game is easy, it's convenient. But how do you think that will work out for you? Why are you giving your power away?

    When you take responsibility for your choices, actions, reactions, and their outcomes, you embrace a powerful role in shaping your life. I promise that when you start taking responsibility you are in control of your life. You have the power to steer your life. You will have self-respect and gain the respect of others. Taking responsibility is a testament to your self-worth. It's a declaration that you are capable of handling life's challenges, learning from them, and emerging stronger.

    By taking responsibility for one's growth and development, you can boost your confidence and self-belief.

2. Embrace Change & Challenges

    Don't fear change and challenges. Every day, the world around us evolves, presenting new scenarios and learning opportunities. Embracing change isn't merely adapting to new circumstances; it's actively engaging with them to foster progress and self-improvement. Consider change as an open door to unexplored possibilities.

    When you shift your perspective to see change and challenges as an ally, it transforms from a source of fear to opportunity. Each challenge overcome is a testament to our capabilities and resilience. It's a means to build self-confidence. By viewing challenges as opportunities to grow, we develop a resilience that equips us to handle future obstacles with greater ease and assurance. Embracing change and challenges is about becoming adaptable.

    Embracing change and challenges fosters adaptability and resilience, helping you overcome fear and seize opportunities for growth.

3. Authenticity

    Be authentic. It's about honouring your true self, your evolving identity, and what genuinely matters to you. Authenticity is the key to unlocking your unique vision and aligning with your core values. Being authentic liberates you from the constraints of societal masks and the exhausting pursuit of living up to others' expectations.

    By being authentic, you:

    a. Shed the masks that hide your true self.
    b. Relinquish the need to pretend, embracing your genuine identity.
    c. Stop the endless cycle of comparing your journey with others.

d. Let go of the pursuit of perfection, understanding that growth and learning are more valuable.

e. Embrace self-acceptance.

Being authentic encourages you to embrace your true self and overcome imposter syndrome, leading to more genuine interactions and confidence.

4. Love

Choose to hold space for love in your heart. When your heart is guided by love, it becomes a reservoir of positive emotions like gratitude, grace, kindness, and compassion — including the crucial practice of self-compassion. Embracing love also fosters empathy, enabling you to understand and connect with others deeply. This loving approach helps dissolve negative emotions such as hatred, resentment, jealousy, and guilt. It replaces regret and shame with understanding and forgiveness. In cultivating a heart full of love, you pave the way for continuous personal growth, emotional resilience, and the ability to positively impact others' lives.

Cultivating empathy, kindness, and compassion for oneself can reduce self-criticism and foster a healthier self-image.

5. Innovate

Be in an Innovative mode. Being in a state of perpetual innovation means actively seeking out knowledge and new experiences. It's about embracing lifelong learning, whether that's through acquiring new skills, pursuing further education, or simply staying curious and open to new ideas.

Self-innovation isn't just about enhancing qualifications; it's a mindset of constant self-renewal and evolution. It's about looking at yourself as a work in progress, always in motion towards becoming a better, more refined version of yourself. This practice goes hand-in-hand with ambition and self-reliance, encouraging you to seize opportunities for self-improvement and growth.

An innovative mindset encourages you to learn and improve without dwelling on mistakes, promoting growth and forward-thinking.

6. Time

Time waits for no one, making it essential to seize the present moment with purpose and intent. Replace procrastination with immediate action, embracing the now as the perfect moment to initiate change and personal growth. Ask yourself, what's holding you back from becoming the best version of yourself? Understand that the right time to start is always now.

Recognizing the value of time also means embracing the power of the present moment. It's about shedding the weight of past experiences and the anxiety of future uncertainties, to focus on the here and now. It's in the present moments that the magic of transformation and personal evolution truly happens. This practice builds self-awareness.

Focusing on the present moment reduces anxiety about the future, allowing us to make better decisions and perform at our best.

7. YOU

Who are YOU? Reflect on who you truly are. When you gaze into the mirror, look beyond the surface. See the unique individual staring back at you, full of potential and possibilities. Ask yourself, what is the essence of your being? What ignites your passion and drives your purpose?

You, in that mirror, are a living testament to the miracle of human potential. Embrace and cherish that. You owe it to yourself to love and honour who you are, to nurture and celebrate your existence. Recognize that you are the master of your destiny. You possess an inner power, an untapped reservoir of strength and capability, ready to transform your life. Believe in your ability to steer your life towards the dreams you aspire to achieve. It's about acknowledging that change starts with you—your decisions, your actions, your commitment to growth.

Practising self-acceptance helps us build self-esteem and a positive self-image, reducing self-doubt and barriers to success.

LOVE YOU! HONOUR YOU! KNOW THAT YOU HAVE THE POWER WITHIN YOU TO TRANSFORM YOUR LIFE.

ONLY YOU CAN TAKE CHARGE AND DIRECT YOUR LIFE IN THE DIRECTION YOU WANT IT TO GO. ONLY YOU CAN MAKE THE CHANGES YOU NEED.

Once you start these new practices, let me tell you something, it's going to be:
  a. Uncomfortable,
  b. Unfamiliar
  c. Uncertain
  d. Unpredictable

Because you are no longer making the same old choices. Instead, you are stretching yourself, you are stepping into your growth zone. You are experiencing the shift.

It's going to be difficult. It's going to be hard. It's going to be unpleasant, but it's going to be worth it.

There was a time in my life when my personal barriers and being trapped in the cycle of self-sabotage continually undermined my potential. When I looked in the mirror, it was as if I was standing in my own shadow, unable to move into the light.

The REALITY Blueprint became my roadmap to transformation.

It wasn't an overnight solution. It required commitment, persistence, and a willingness to confront the uncomfortable. I started by taking Responsibility for my life – no longer blaming circumstances or others for my unhappiness. Embracing Change and being adaptable became a mantra, as I learned to view challenges as opportunities for growth rather than insurmountable obstacles.

Authenticity was perhaps my greatest struggle, but also my most rewarding victory. I peeled back the layers of who I thought I should be, and how I should be living my life, revealing my true self, and in doing so, found my voice and my path. I discovered the powers within self-acceptance. Love and compassion, both for myself and others, healed old wounds and opened my heart to gratitude and kindness.

Personal innovation and a continuous improvement mindset propelled me forward, breaking the shackles of complacency. I embraced Time as a precious resource, learning the art of mindfulness, and understanding that the present moment was the only time to act, grow, and live.

Finally, honouring myself was about acknowledging my worth, celebrating my journey, and recognizing that the person in the mirror deserved the same love and respect I gave to others. This element was about coming full circle, from self-sabotage to self-love. Its about shifting my mindset from I am a victim to I am master and leader of my life.

Today, as I reflect on my journey, I see it not as a series of steps but as a dance – sometimes slow and steady, sometimes brisk and challenging, but always moving towards a life of purpose, fulfillment, and mindset-mastery. The R.E.A.L.I.T.Y Blueprint was and still is my guide, my personal mentor.

My hope is to inspire you to embark on your own journey of transformation, with the knowledge that while the path isn't easy, I promise you, the destination of mastering and leading one's life is profoundly worth it.

Reality is a mirror, Reflect the powerful you!

Notes

The Commitment

What is it that we want in life? At the heart of our desires lies a universal longing–the quest for happiness, success, and a fulfilling life.

But how do we transform these aspirations into tangible realities?

The answer lies in a pivotal shift: moving from the shadows of self-sabotage to the empowering light of self-leadership through cultivating a growth mindset.

This transformative journey is navigated through the guiding principles of the R.E.A.L.I.T.Y. Blueprint, the GPS for creating the reality of your heart's desire.

SELF-SABOTAGE

Blame, Victim mindset, complaining, a passenger of life, life happens to me

Fear of change & challenges

Living life based on other people's expectations, people pleasing, comparing, lack of self-acceptance

Resentment, grudge, jealousy, hatred, shame, regret

Lack of self-belief, I can't attitude, negative self-talk

Focused on and living in the past and anxious about the future

Lack of self-respect, self-honour and self-love

SELF-LEADERSHIP

Responsibility - taking personal responsibility of ones life. Being in the drivers seat

Embrace change and challenges - overcome fear

Authenticity - being authentic, practice self-acceptance and set your own standard

Love - hold space for love in your heart. Therein lies kindness, compassion, gratitude

Innovative mode - seek for continuous improvement. Have a can do attitude. Have self belief.

Time - it waits for no one and magic happens in the NOW. Live in the Present

You - the person in the mirror. Honour and respect YOU. Meet the needs of the 5yr old and 8oyr old in you. Whats your legacy going to be?

Embrace these seven core principles as your compass, leading you to discover and harness your true potential. These are not abstract concepts but actionable paths to your desired life.

Your commitment to practice and integrate these seven principles in your daily life is about you charting a course towards a future where every step is an advancement towards your goals, every decision a reflection of your deepest values, and every moment an opportunity to realise the extraordinary potential of your life.

Setting an Intention–Vision & Goals using the 'WOOP' Method

The practice of setting intentions is a powerful catalyst for personal and professional growth. Unlike passive hopes or wishes, intentions are active commitments to ourselves, they guide our thoughts, emotions, behaviours, and actions towards a desired outcome.

When we set intentions, we do more than just outline what we want to achieve; we also establish how we want to live our lives, make decisions, and interact with the world around us. Setting intentions is about manifesting the life we envision. It's a practice that encourages mindfulness, responsibility, and active engagement with our dreams.

One effective way of setting an intention is the WOOP Method–Wish, Outcome, Obstacle, Plan–a technique introduced by *Gabriele Oettingen* (a leading scientist in the field of motivation and goal attainment), in her book, *Rethinking Positive Thinking*. It is based on scientific goal setting, motivation, and visualisation research. It is designed to help individuals set and achieve their goals more effectively.

It is a method that provides a structured approach to not only set goals but also to foresee potential challenges and develop actionable plans to overcome them. It's a tool that transforms mere aspirations into achievable objectives. As we know, success isn't just about wishful thinking. It's equally important to identify potential obstacles that could hinder your progress. This realistic assessment helps you prepare for challenges, making your plan more resilient. Finally, it will require you to devise a plan–a specific action or a set of actions that will help you overcome these obstacles and move closer to your vision and goals. This plan should be concrete, practical, and actionable.

Setting an intention is the first step in turning the invisible into the visible, the foundation upon which all dreams are built and realised.

How to Set an Intention Using the
WOOP Method – Vision & Goals

Step 1: WISH

The first step in creating WOOP goals is to identify your wish, which is your ultimate goal. This step involves asking yourself, 'What do I really want?' and determining what you most want to achieve.

When identifying your wish, it's important to be as specific as possible. A vague or unclear goal can make creating a concrete plan for achieving it difficult. Additionally, choosing a challenging but realistic goal is vital so you can feel a sense of accomplishment when you reach it. It's not just about wishful thinking, it's about truly believing in and visualising your goals and then taking action towards them.

When completing this step, it can be helpful to consider the following questions:

- What is the vision I see for myself? (Use visualisation techniques here)
- What would make me happiest or most fulfilled?
- What do I really care about?
- What is the most important thing I want to achieve right now?

Step 2: OUTCOME

The second step in the WOOP technique is identifying the positive outcome of achieving your goal. This step involves asking yourself, 'Why do I want to achieve this goal?' and determining what will make achieving your goal worthwhile.

What's the best possible outcome that would result from accomplishing your goal? How would you feel? Visualise this outcome in your mind. When identifying your outcome, it would be best to be being as specific as possible. This will help you stay motivated and focused on your goal when obstacles arise. Additionally, choosing a meaningful and personally relevant outcome is vital to stay motivated to achieve it.

When completing this step, it can be helpful to consider the following questions:

- What will be the benefits of achieving my goal?
- What positive feelings or experiences will I have when I reach my goal?
- How will achieving my goal improve my life?
- How will achieving this goal impact the people around me?

Step 3: OBSTACLE

The third step in creating WOOP goals is to identify the obstacles that stand in your way. This step involves asking yourself, 'What is preventing me from achieving my goal?' and identifying the things that might hinder your success.

What's standing in the way between you and your goal? Visualise this obstacle in your mind.

When identifying your obstacles, being honest with yourself is essential. Identifying potential obstacles can help you prepare for them and create a plan for overcoming them. Additionally, it's vital to be realistic about your obstacles. This will help you create a program that is both achievable and effective.

When completing this step, it can be helpful to consider the following questions:
- What challenges or barriers might I face when trying to achieve my goal?
- What are the biggest obstacles that stand in my way?
- What could prevent me from achieving my goal?
- Is there anyone who will stop me?

Step 4: PLAN

The final step in the WOOP technique is to create a plan for overcoming the obstacles and achieving your goal. This step involves asking yourself, 'What steps can I take to achieve my goal?' and creating a concrete plan for taking action.

Make a plan for overcoming your obstacle. What action would help you when your obstacle shows up? Create an if/then plan and visualise it in your mind. If / When _____ (obstacle), then I will _____ (action to overcome obstacle).

When creating your plan, it's crucial to be as specific and actionable. This will help you stay on track and make progress toward your goal.

Additionally, flexibility and adaptability are necessary as unexpected obstacles or challenges arise. By creating a plan that is both realistic and flexible, you can increase your chances of success.

When completing this step, it can be helpful to consider the following questions:
- What specific actions can I take to overcome the obstacles I've identified?
- What resources do I need to achieve my goal?
- What steps will I take to measure my progress and track my success?
- What tools can I use to keep me on track with my plans?

Here is a Simple Example of How You Could Start Using WOOP in Your Own Life.

Goal: Improved leadership at work

Wish

I want to improve my leadership skills and become a better manager.

Outcome

If I become a better leader, I can be more effective, motivate and inspire my team and achieve better results for the organization.

Obstacle

Becoming a leader will mean an increase in workload. I find it hard to delegate tasks and often feel I need to be in control and do everything myself.

Plan

I will identify tasks that can be assigned to others, communicate my expectations clearly, and provide support and feedback to my team to help them succeed.

My transformation journey to change began with a simple, yet crucial step: setting a clear intention to turn my life around. It was a moment of profound clarity, where I consciously decided to change the course of my life, to break free from the cycles of self-doubt and to lead a life filled with purpose. My desired outcome was to be a more confident and fulfilled version of myself. I would create vision boards and write in my journal.

I didn't, however, have the privilege of the WOOP method before.

However, these days, I turn to the WOOP tool for goal setting. With WOOP, I can meticulously craft a plan, address obstacles with specific strategies and actions. This method isn't just about a hope or a dream; it's about creating a practical roadmap to turn my intentions into reality.

This method is powerful because, it will teach you to not only envision a goal but also actively plan for its challenges. It's a realistic and grounded way to get on a path of your journey of transformation and to start crafting your new reality.

'WOOP' Your Goal

WISH - What do I really want?

OUTCOME - Why do I want to achieve this goal?

OBSTACLES - What could prevent me from achieving my goal?

Plan - What steps can I take to achieve my goal?

Notes

The Daily Journal & Weekly Review

You will use the following section to record your daily practice of the seven core principles. At the end of the week there will be a weekly check-in.

You will also practice a daily gratitude. Incorporating gratitude into daily life is important because it fundamentally shifts how we perceive and interact with the world around us. Gratitude is highly valued because it encompasses feelings of appreciation, humility, and acknowledgment of the positive aspects of life, both big and small. The impact and benefits of this practice are both psychological and physiological, profoundly influencing our overall well-being.

Daily Journal - Example   **Date:**

Innovation distinguishes between a leader and a follower. – Steve Jobs

My Morning Prompt

Today, I will look for ways to improve who I am and what I do by:
(Write down your thoughts, feelings, and actions).
Today, I will look for ways to improve who I am and what I do by practising mindfulness in my interactions and tasks. I've noticed lately that I've been quite distracted and not fully present, whether it's during conversations with friends or while working on projects. My mind seems to wander, thinking about what's next on my to-do list or replaying past events.

I am grateful for... *(Practice daily gratitude)*
I am grateful for *my job. While it can be challenging at times, it provides me with a sense of purpose, opportunities for growth, and the ability to support myself and contribute to the lives of others. It's more than a job; it's a part of my journey that teaches me new lessons every day.*

Daily Identity Affirmation:

Every decision I make is a choice that shapes my reality and my future.

Daily Worldview Affirmation:

I am connected to the universe, and this connection guides me to manifest my reality.

[Nb: The real power behind affirmations: You have to believe them; you have to feel them, and you have to live them.]

My Evening Reflections:

What specific actions did I take to proactively be mindful at work today?

During conversations, I made a conscious effort to listen actively, not just hear. This means putting away my phone, making eye contact, and really absorbing what the other person is saying without mentally preparing my response.

How did these actions relate to my effort to improve things and what did I learn?

These actions demonstrated my commitment to being more mindful by actively engaging in the present moment.

I learned that my conscious effort to improve my presence and awareness directly contributes to my goal of personal improvement and mindfulness.

Highlights of the day:

1. *During meetings today, I made a conscious effort to listen actively, fully absorbing the discussions without rushing to respond. This not only helped me understand my colleagues' perspectives better but also allowed me to contribute more thoughtfully.*

2. *I approached my tasks with full attention, minimizing multitasking. This focus made my work more efficient and enjoyable, and I found that I made fewer errors and felt less stressed by the end of the day.*

The moment you take responsibility for everything in your life is
the moment you can change anything in your life. – Hal Elrod

My Morning Prompt

Today, I will take responsibility for my life and career by...
(Write down your thoughts, feelings, and actions).

I am grateful for... *(Practice daily gratitude)*

Daily Identity Affirmation:

I am the architect of my life; my choices and actions shape my future.

Daily Worldview Affirmation:

Every interaction is an opportunity to learn, grow, and contribute positively.

[Nb: The real power behind affirmations: You have to believe them;
you have to feel them, and you have to live them.]

My Evening Reflections:

What specific actions did I take to proactively shape my
professional and personal life today?

How did these actions make me feel more in control and
empowered and what did I learn?

Highlights of the day:

Change is the law of life, and those who look only to the past or present are certain to miss the future. – John F. Kennedy

My Morning Prompt

Today, I will embrace change and take on challenges by...
(Write down your thoughts, feelings, and actions).

I am grateful for... *(Practice daily gratitude)*

Daily Identity Affirmation:

The power to change my world lies within me; I use it wisely and with intention.

Daily Worldview Affirmation:

The world conspires in my favour, aligning circumstances for my highest good.

[Nb: The real power behind affirmations: You have to believe them; you have to feel them, and you have to live them.]

My Evening Reflections:

What specific actions did I take to proactively shape
my professional and personal life today?

How did these actions make me feel more open to change and
challenges as stepping stones and what did I learn?

Highlights of the day:

Your time is limited, don't waste it living someone else's life. – Steve Jobs

My Morning Prompt

Today, I will embrace being authentic and honour my true self by... *(Write down your thoughts, feelings, and actions).*

I am grateful for... *(Practice daily gratitude)*

Daily Identity Affirmation:

I am the author of my story and write each chapter with purpose and passion.

Daily Worldview Affirmation:

My actions are in harmony with the universe, co-creating my desired future.

[Nb: The real power behind affirmations: You have to believe them; you have to feel them, and you have to live them.]

What specific actions did I take to proactively shape
my professional and personal life today?

How did these actions make me feel more authentic
and empowered and what did I learn?

Highlights of the day:

Love and compassion are necessities, not luxuries. Without them, humanity cannot survive. – Dalai Lama

My Morning Prompt

Today, I will hold space for love in my heart and practice self-compassion by... *(Write down your thoughts, feelings, and actions).*

I am grateful for... *(Practice daily gratitude)*

Daily Identity Affirmation:

I trust in my ability to create a fulfilling and meaningful life experience.

Daily Worldview Affirmation:

I am an active participant in creating a compassionate and thriving world.

[Nb: The real power behind affirmations: You have to believe them; you have to feel them, and you have to live them.]

What specific actions did I take to proactively shape my
professional and personal life today?

How did these actions make me practice self-compassion and what did I learn?

Highlights of the day:

Innovation distinguishes between a leader and a follower. – Steve Jobs

My Morning Prompt

Today, I will look for ways to improve who I am and what I
do by... *(Write down your thoughts, feelings, and actions).*

I am grateful for... *(Practice daily gratitude)*

Daily Identity Affirmation:

Every decision I make is a choice that shapes my reality and my future.

Daily Worldview Affirmation:

I am connected to the universe, and this connection guides me to manifest my reality.

[Nb: The real power behind affirmations: You have to believe them;
you have to feel them, and you have to live them.]

My Evening Reflections:

What specific actions did I take to proactively shape my professional and personal life today?

How did these actions relate my effort to improve things and what did I learn?

Highlights of the day:

"The present moment is filled with joy and happiness. If you are attentive, you will see it." - Thich Nhat Hanh"

My Morning Prompt

Today, I will focus on the present instead of dwelling on the past or being anxious of the future by... *(Write down your thoughts, feelings, and actions).*

I am grateful for... *(Practice daily gratitude)*

Daily Identity Affirmation:

Every moment in time is an opportunity to create the life I desire.

Daily Worldview Affirmation:

My dreams and goals are right here within reach, as I actively work to receive them.

[Nb: The real power behind affirmations: You have to believe them; you have to feel them, and you have to live them.]

What specific actions did I take to be more self-aware
and focus on the present moment today?

How did these actions allow me to create magic in
the present time and what did I learn?

Highlights of the day:

You yourself, as much as anybody in the entire universe,
deserve your love and affection. – Buddha

My Morning Prompt

Today, I will practice self-love and self-acceptance and I will honour
myself by... *(Write down your thoughts, feelings, and actions).*

I am grateful for... *(Practice daily gratitude)*

Daily Identity Affirmation:

I am worthy of happiness, success, and fulfilment."

Daily Worldview Affirmation:

Everything happens at the right time and according to the divine plan.

[Nb: The real power behind affirmations: You have to believe them;
you have to feel them, and you have to live them.]

My Evening Reflections:

What specific actions did I take to proactively shape
my professional and personal life today?

How did these actions allow me to honour and accept
myself for who I am and what did I learn?

Highlights of the day:

Weekly Check-Ins

1. A section to summarise your progress, record any setbacks, and lessons learned during the week.
2. Space for resetting specific goals related to each principle for the upcoming week.

What was the most significant lesson I learned about myself this week?

How have the seven principles guided my behaviour,
decisions and actions this week?

What do I want to focus on or improve in the upcoming week?

Notes

Success is not final, failure is not fatal: It is the courage
to continue that counts. – Winston Churchill

My Morning Prompt

Today, I will take responsibility for my life and career by...
(Write down your thoughts, feelings, and actions).

I am grateful for... *(Practice daily gratitude)*

Daily Identity Affirmation:

I am accountable for my journey and embrace each step with courage.

Daily Worldview Affirmation:

My perspective shapes my experience; I choose a positive and empowering viewpoint.

[Nb: The real power behind affirmations: You have to believe them;
you have to feel them, and you have to live them.]

What specific actions did I take to proactively shape
my professional and personal life today?

How did these actions make me feel more in control
and empowered and what did I learn?

Highlights of the day:

The only way to make sense out of change is to plunge into it, move with it, and join the dance. – Alan Watts

My Morning Prompt

Today, I will embrace change and take on challenges by...
(Write down your thoughts, feelings, and actions).

I am grateful for... *(Practice daily gratitude)*

Daily Identity Affirmation:

I embrace change with an open heart and mind, knowing each challenge is a stepping stone to growth.

Daily Worldview Affirmation:

My dreams and goals are in alignment to what the universe has in store for me.

[Nb: The real power behind affirmations: You have to believe them; you have to feel them, and you have to live them.]

My Evening Reflections:

What specific actions did I take to proactively shape
my professional and personal life today?

How did these actions make me feel more open to change and
challenges as stepping stones and what did I learn?

Highlights of the day:

Authenticity is a collection of choices that we have to make every day.
It's about the choice to show up and be real. – Brené Brown

My Morning Prompt

Today, I will embrace being authentic and honour my true
self by... *(Write down your thoughts, feelings, and actions).*

I am grateful for... *(Practice daily gratitude)*

Daily Identity Affirmation:

I am true to myself in all that I do, and my authenticity shines in every action I take.

Daily Worldview Affirmation:

I am connected to the universe, and this connection guides me to manifest my reality.

[Nb: The real power behind affirmations: You have to believe them;
you have to feel them, and you have to live them.]

My Evening Reflections:

What specific actions did I take to proactively shape
my professional and personal life today?

How did these actions make me feel more authentic
and empowered and what did I learn?

Highlights of the day:

Love and compassion are the truest forms of strength. – Daisaku Ikeda

My Morning Prompt

Today, I will hold space for love in my heart and practice self-compassion by...*(Write down your thoughts, feelings, and actions).*

I am grateful for... *(Practice daily gratitude)*

Daily Identity Affirmation:

I lead with love and compassion, enriching my life and the lives of others.

Daily Worldview Affirmation:

Positive energy surrounds me; I attract uplifting and empowering experiences.

[Nb: The real power behind affirmations: You have to believe them; you have to feel them, and you have to live them.]

What specific actions did I take to proactively shape
my professional and personal life today?

How did these actions make me practice self-compassion and what did I learn?

Highlights of the day:

Continuous improvement is better than delayed perfection. – Mark Twain

My Morning Prompt

Today, I will look for ways to improve who I am and what I do by... *(Write down your thoughts, feelings, and actions).*

I am grateful for... *(Practice daily gratitude)*

Daily Identity Affirmation:

I am a perpetual learner, embracing innovation and creativity as keys to my growth.

Daily Worldview Affirmation:

I am surrounded by endless opportunities that enrich my journey.

[Nb: The real power behind affirmations: You have to believe them; you have to feel them, and you have to live them.]

What specific actions did I take to proactively shape
my professional and personal life today?

How did these actions relate my effort to improve things and what did I learn?

Highlights of the day:

The secret of health for both mind and body is not to mourn for the past,
not to worry about the future, or not to anticipate troubles, but to
live in the present moment wisely and earnestly. – Buddha

My Morning Prompt

Today, I will focus on the present instead of dwelling on the past or being anxious of the future by... *(Write down your thoughts, feelings, and actions).*

I am grateful for... *(Practice daily gratitude)*

Daily Identity Affirmation:

I live each moment fully, honouring myself with love, respect, and care.

Daily Worldview Affirmation:

The universe is abundant, and its generosity flows into my life.

[Nb: The real power behind affirmations: You have to believe them; you have to feel them, and you have to live them.]

What specific actions did I take to be more self-aware
and focus on the present moment today?

How did these actions allow me to create magic in the present
time and what did I learn?

Highlights of the day:

*The most powerful relationship you will ever have is the
relationship with yourself. – Steve Maraboli*

My Morning Prompt

Today, I will practice self-love and self-acceptance, and I will honour
myself by... *(Write down your thoughts, feelings, and actions).*

I am grateful for... *(Practice daily gratitude)*

Daily Identity Affirmation:

I possess the power to create the life I envision for myself.

Daily Worldview Affirmation:

I trust the journey of life, knowing each step unfolds with purpose and meaning.

[Nb: The real power behind affirmations: You have to believe them;
you have to feel them, and you have to live them.]

My Evening Reflections:

What specific actions did I take to proactively shape
my professional and personal life today?

How did these actions allow me to honour and accept
myself for who I am and what did I learn?

Highlights of the day:

Weekly Check-Ins

1. A section to summarise your progress, record any setbacks, and lessons learned during the week.
2. Space for resetting specific goals related to each principle for the upcoming week.

What was the most significant lesson I learned about myself this week?

How have the seven principles guided my behaviour, decisions and actions this week?

What do I want to focus on or improve in the upcoming week?

Notes

Owning our story and loving ourselves through that process is the
bravest thing that we will ever do. – Brené Brown

My Morning Prompt

Today, I will take responsibility for my life and career by...
(Write down your thoughts, feelings, and actions).

I am grateful for... *(Practice daily gratitude)*

Daily Identity Affirmation:

I am in control of my actions and responsible for their outcomes.

Daily Worldview Affirmation:

My choices reflect my values and desires, steering me towards my goals.

[Nb: The real power behind affirmations: You have to believe them;
you have to feel them, and you have to live them.]

My Evening Reflections:

What specific actions did I take to proactively shape
my professional and personal life today?

How did these actions make me feel more in control
and empowered and what did I learn?

Highlights of the day:

The power to change anything in your life is in the
decisions you make today. – Darren Hardy

My Morning Prompt

Today, I will embrace change and take on challenges by...
(Write down your thoughts, feelings, and actions).

I am grateful for... *(Practice daily gratitude)*

Daily Identity Affirmation:

I embrace change as a natural part of the creative process of life.

Daily Worldview Affirmation:

I view challenges as chances to manifest my strength and creativity.

[Nb: The real power behind affirmations: You have to believe them;
you have to feel them, and you have to live them.]

What specific actions did I take to proactively shape
my professional and personal life today?

How did these actions make me feel more open to change and
challenges as stepping stones and what did I learn?

Highlights of the day:

To be yourself in a world that is constantly trying to make you something else is the greatest accomplishment. – Ralph Waldo Emerson

My Morning Prompt

Today, I will embrace being authentic and honour my true self by... *(Write down your thoughts, feelings, and actions).*

I am grateful for... *(Practice daily gratitude)*

Daily Identity Affirmation:

I am true to myself in all that I do, and my authenticity shines in every action I take.

Daily Worldview Affirmation:

My dreams and goals are within reach, as I actively work to realise them.

[Nb: The real power behind affirmations: You have to believe them; you have to feel them, and you have to live them.]

My Evening Reflections:

What specific actions did I take to proactively shape
my professional and personal life today?

How did these actions make me feel more authentic
and empowered and what did I learn?

Highlights of the day:

To fall in love with yourself is the first secret to happiness. – Robert Morley

My Morning Prompt

Today, I will hold space for love in my heart and practice self-compassion by... *(Write down your thoughts, feelings, and actions).*

I am grateful for... *(Practice daily gratitude)*

Daily Identity Affirmation:

I am a harmonious blend of wisdom, compassion, and assertiveness.

Daily Worldview Affirmation:

The world conspires in my favour, aligning circumstances for my highest good.

[Nb: The real power behind affirmations: You have to believe them; you have to feel them, and you have to live them.]

My Evening Reflections:

What specific actions did I take to proactively shape
my professional and personal life today?

How did these actions make me practice self-compassion and what did I learn?

Highlights of the day:

Growth and comfort do not coexist. – Ginni Rometty

My Morning Prompt

Today, I will look for ways to improve who I am and what I do by... *(Write down your thoughts, feelings, and actions).*

I am grateful for... *(Practice daily gratitude)*

Daily Identity Affirmation:

I am a beacon of creativity and innovation, constantly evolving and growing.

Daily Worldview Affirmation:

The universe collaborates with my dreams, creating a tapestry of success and fulfilment.

[Nb: The real power behind affirmations: You have to believe them; you have to feel them, and you have to live them.]

My Evening Reflections:

What specific actions did I take to proactively shape
my professional and personal life today?

How did these actions relate my effort to improve things and what did I learn?

Highlights of the day:

Do not wait until the conditions are perfect to begin.
Beginning makes the conditions perfect. – Alan Cohen

My Morning Prompt

Today, I will focus on the present instead of dwelling on the past or being anxious of the future by... *(Write down your thoughts, feelings, and actions).*

I am grateful for... *(Practice daily gratitude)*

Daily Identity Affirmation:

I am the master of my fate, and every day, I move closer to my ideal future.

Daily Worldview Affirmation:

I navigate life's flow with ease and grace, trusting in the universe's wise timing.

[Nb: The real power behind affirmations: You have to believe them;
you have to feel them, and you have to live them.]

My Evening Reflections:

What specific actions did I take to be more self-aware
and focus on the present moment today?

How did these actions allow me to create magic in
the present time and what did I learn?

Highlights of the day:

The most terrifying thing is to accept oneself completely. – Carl Jung

My Morning Prompt

Today, I will practice self-love and self-acceptance, and I will honour myself by... *(Write down your thoughts, feelings, and actions).*

I am grateful for... *(Practice daily gratitude)*

Daily Identity Affirmation:

I am deeply rooted in self-love and self-respect.

Daily Worldview Affirmation:

My connection with the universe shows me a world full of beauty, wonder, and possibilities.

[Nb: The real power behind affirmations: You have to believe them; you have to feel them, and you have to live them.]

My Evening Reflections:

What specific actions did I take to proactively shape
my professional and personal life today?

How did these actions allow me to honour and accept
myself for who I am and what did I learn?

Highlights of the day:

Weekly Check-Ins

1. A section to summarise your progress, record any setbacks, and lessons learned during the week.

2. Space for resetting specific goals related to each principle for the upcoming week.

What was the most significant lesson I learned about myself this week?

How have the seven principles guided my behaviour,
decisions and actions this week?

What do I want to focus on or improve in the upcoming week?

Notes

Self-respect, self-worth, and self-love, all start with self. Stop
looking outside of yourself for your value. – Rob Liano

My Morning Prompt

Today, I will take responsibility for my life and career by...
(Write down your thoughts, feelings, and actions).

I am grateful for... *(Practice daily gratitude)*

Daily Identity Affirmation:

I am a champion of my own story, courageous in writing every chapter.

Daily Worldview Affirmation:

My perspective shapes my experience; I choose a positive and empowering viewpoint.

[Nb: The real power behind affirmations: You have to believe them;
you have to feel them, and you have to live them.]

My Evening Reflections:

What specific actions did I take to proactively shape
my professional and personal life today?

How did these actions make me feel more in control
and empowered and what did I learn?

Highlights of the day:

Change is the law of life, and those who look only to the past or present are certain to miss the future. – John F. Kennedy

My Morning Prompt

Today, I will embrace change and take on challenges by...
(Write down your thoughts, feelings, and actions).

I am grateful for... *(Practice daily gratitude)*

Daily Identity Affirmation:

I am an agent of change, transforming my life with purpose and passion.

Daily Worldview Affirmation:

The power to change my world lies within me; I use it wisely and with intention.

[Nb: The real power behind affirmations: You have to believe them; you have to feel them, and you have to live them.]

What specific actions did I take to proactively shape
my professional and personal life today?

How did these actions make me feel more open to change and
challenges as stepping stones and what did I learn?

Highlights of the day:

The greatest thing in the world is to know how to
belong to oneself. – Michel de Montaigne

My Morning Prompt

Today, I will embrace being authentic and honour my true
self by... *(Write down your thoughts, feelings, and actions).*

I am grateful for... *(Practice daily gratitude)*

Daily Identity Affirmation:

I am deeply connected to my inner wisdom, guiding me towards my truth.

Daily Worldview Affirmation:

I witness the unfolding of my life's path with awe and appreciation, embracing each
new dawn.

[Nb: The real power behind affirmations: You have to believe them;
you have to feel them, and you have to live them.]

What specific actions did I take to proactively shape
my professional and personal life today?

How did these actions make me feel more authentic
and empowered and what did I learn?

Highlights of the day:

You yourself, as much as anybody in the entire universe,
deserve your love and affection. – Buddha

My Morning Prompt

Today, I will hold space for love in my heart and practice self-compassion by... *(Write down your thoughts, feelings, and actions).*

I am grateful for... *(Practice daily gratitude)*

Daily Identity Affirmation:

I am a source of love, inspiration and positivity to myself and those around me.

Daily Worldview Affirmation:

I see the world through a lens of compassion and gratitude, recognizing the beauty that surrounds me.

[Nb: The real power behind affirmations: You have to believe them; you have to feel them, and you have to live them.]

My Evening Reflections:

What specific actions did I take to proactively shape
my professional and personal life today?

How did these actions make me practice self-compassion and what did I learn?

Highlights of the day:

Personal development is the belief that you are worth the effort,
time, and energy needed to develop yourself. – Denis Waitley

My Morning Prompt

Today, I will look for ways to improve who I am and what I
do by... *(Write down your thoughts, feelings, and actions).*

I am grateful for... *(Practice daily gratitude)*

Daily Identity Affirmation:

I am a wellspring of creativity, constantly birthing new ideas and perspectives.

Daily Worldview Affirmation:

I contribute to the world's harmony, my presence a soothing melody in the symphony
of life.

[Nb: The real power behind affirmations: You have to believe them;
you have to feel them, and you have to live them.]

My Evening Reflections:

What specific actions did I take to proactively shape
my professional and personal life today?

How did these actions relate my effort to improve things and what did I learn?

Highlights of the day:

Be not afraid of growing slowly, be afraid only of standing still. – Chinese Proverb

My Morning Prompt

Today, I will focus on the present instead of dwelling on the past or being anxious of the future by... *(Write down your thoughts, feelings, and actions).*

I am grateful for... *(Practice daily gratitude)*

Daily Identity Affirmation:

I shape my destiny with confidence and clarity, each day a step closer to my purpose.

Daily Worldview Affirmation:

My actions are intentional, and they create a positive impact in my world.

[Nb: The real power behind affirmations: You have to believe them; you have to feel them, and you have to live them.]

What specific actions did I take to be more self-aware
and focus on the present moment today?

How did these actions allow me to create magic in
the present time and what did I learn?

Highlights of the day:

The best way to predict your future is to create it. – Peter Drucker

My Morning Prompt

Today, I will practice self-love and self-acceptance, and I will honour myself by... *(Write down your thoughts, feelings, and actions).*

I am grateful for... *(Practice daily gratitude)*

Daily Identity Affirmation:

I am a force of positivity, influencing my surroundings with my light.

Daily Worldview Affirmation:

The universe surrounds me with a circle of positive influence that attracts supportive empowering energies towards me.

[Nb: The real power behind affirmations: You have to believe them; you have to feel them, and you have to live them.]

What specific actions did I take to proactively shape
my professional and personal life today?

How did these actions allow me to honour and accept
myself for who I am and what did I learn?

Highlights of the day:

Weekly Check-Ins

1. A section to summarise your progress, record any setbacks, and lessons learned during the week.

2. Space for resetting specific goals related to each principle for the upcoming week.

What was the most significant lesson I learned about myself this week?

How have the seven principles guided my behaviour, decisions and actions this week?

What do I want to focus on or improve in the upcoming week?

Notes

You must take personal responsibility. You cannot change the circumstances, the seasons, or the wind, but you can change yourself. – Jim Rohn

My Morning Prompt

Today, I will take responsibility for my life and career by...
(Write down your thoughts, feelings, and actions).

I am grateful for... *(Practice daily gratitude)*

Daily Identity Affirmation:

I am accountable for my journey and embrace each step with courage.

Daily Worldview Affirmation:

The universe collaborates with my dreams, creating a tapestry of success and fulfilment.

[Nb: The real power behind affirmations: You have to believe them; you have to feel them, and you have to live them.]

My Evening Reflections:

What specific actions did I take to proactively shape
my professional and personal life today?

How did these actions make me feel more in control
and empowered and what did I learn?

Highlights of the day:

The only way to make sense out of change is to plunge into
it, move with it, and join the dance. – Alan Watts

My Morning Prompt

Today, I will embrace change and take on challenges by...
(Write down your thoughts, feelings, and actions).

I am grateful for... *(Practice daily gratitude)*

Daily Identity Affirmation:

I embrace change as a natural part of the creative process of life.

Daily Worldview Affirmation:

The power to change my world lies within me; I use it wisely and with intention.

[Nb: The real power behind affirmations: You have to believe them;
you have to feel them, and you have to live them.]

What specific actions did I take to proactively shape
my professional and personal life today?

How did these actions make me feel more open to change and
challenges as stepping stones and what did I learn?

Highlights of the day:

Be who you are and say what you feel, because those who mind don't matter, and those who matter don't mind. - Bernard M. Baruch

My Morning Prompt

Today, I will embrace being authentic and honour my true self by... *(Write down your thoughts, feelings, and actions).*

I am grateful for... *(Practice daily gratitude)*

Daily Identity Affirmation:

I am deeply connected to my inner wisdom, guiding me towards my truth.

Daily Worldview Affirmation:

I witness the unfolding of my life's path with awe and appreciation, embracing each new dawn.

[Nb: The real power behind affirmations: You have to believe them; you have to feel them, and you have to live them.]

What specific actions did I take to proactively shape
my professional and personal life today?

How did these actions make me feel more authentic
and empowered and what did I learn?

Highlights of the day:

Love is the only force capable of transforming an enemy
into a friend. – Martin Luther King Jr.

My Morning Prompt

Today, I will hold space for love in my heart and practice self-compassion by... *(Write down your thoughts, feelings, and actions).*

I am grateful for... *(Practice daily gratitude)*

Daily Identity Affirmation:

I am a vessel of love, spreading kindness and compassion.

Daily Worldview Affirmation:

The universe amplifies the love I give and brings it back to me manifold.

[Nb: The real power behind affirmations: You have to believe them; you have to feel them, and you have to live them.]

My Evening Reflections:

What specific actions did I take to proactively shape
my professional and personal life today?

How did these actions make me practice self-compassion and what did I learn?

Highlights of the day:

The true sign of intelligence is not knowledge but imagination. – Albert Einstein

My Morning Prompt

Today, I will look for ways to improve who I am and what I do by... *(Write down your thoughts, feelings, and actions).*

I am grateful for... *(Practice daily gratitude)*

Daily Identity Affirmation:

I am innovative, always seeking new ways to grow and improve.

Daily Worldview Affirmation:

The universe responds to my innovative ideas with opportunities and resources.

[Nb: The real power behind affirmations: You have to believe them; you have to feel them, and you have to live them.]

My Evening Reflections:

What specific actions did I take to proactively shape
my professional and personal life today?

How did these actions relate my effort to improve things and what did I learn?

Highlights of the day:

Realise deeply that the present moment is all you ever have. Make
the Now the primary focus of your life. – Eckhart Tolle

My Morning Prompt

Today, I will focus on the present instead of dwelling on the past or being anxious of the future by... *(Write down your thoughts, feelings, and actions).*

I am grateful for... *(Practice daily gratitude)*

Daily Identity Affirmation:

I am present, fully experiencing each moment as it unfolds.

Daily Worldview Affirmation:

The universe aligns with my mindful moments, enhancing my clarity and focus.

[Nb: The real power behind affirmations: You have to believe them; you have to feel them, and you have to live them.]

My Evening Reflections:

What specific actions did I take to be more self-aware
and focus on the present moment today?

How did these actions allow me to create magic in
the present time and what did I learn?

Highlights of the day:

To love oneself is the beginning of a lifelong romance. – Oscar Wilde

My Morning Prompt

Today, I will practice self-love and self-acceptance, and I will honour myself by... *(Write down your thoughts, feelings, and actions).*

I am grateful for... *(Practice daily gratitude)*

Daily Identity Affirmation:

I am self-loving, nurturing a positive and caring relationship with myself.

Daily Worldview Affirmation:

As I honour myself, the universe reflects back respect and worthiness.

[Nb: The real power behind affirmations: You have to believe them; you have to feel them, and you have to live them.]

My Evening Reflections:

What specific actions did I take to proactively shape
my professional and personal life today?

How did these actions allow me to honour and accept
myself for who I am and what did I learn?

Highlights of the day:

Weekly Check-Ins

1. A section to summarise your progress, record any setbacks, and lessons learned during the week.
2. Space for resetting specific goals related to each principle for the upcoming week.

What was the most significant lesson I learned about myself this week?

How have the seven principles guided my behaviour,
decisions and actions this week?

What do I want to focus on or improve in the upcoming week?

Notes

The price of greatness is responsibility. – Winston Churchill

My Morning Prompt

Today, I will take responsibility for my life and career by...
(Write down your thoughts, feelings, and actions).

I am grateful for... *(Practice daily gratitude)*

Daily Identity Affirmation:

I am accountable for my actions and their impact on my life.

Daily Worldview Affirmation:

Every step I take in responsibility aligns me with the universe's path of abundance.

[Nb: The real power behind affirmations: You have to believe them;
you have to feel them, and you have to live them.]

What specific actions did I take to proactively shape
my professional and personal life today?

How did these actions make me feel more in control
and empowered and what did I learn?

Highlights of the day:

It is not the strongest of the species that survive, nor the most intelligent,
but the one most responsive to change. – Charles Darwin

My Morning Prompt

Today, I will embrace change and take on challenges by...
(Write down your thoughts, feelings, and actions).

I am grateful for... *(Practice daily gratitude)*

Daily Identity Affirmation:

I am adaptable, embracing change as an opportunity for growth.

Daily Worldview Affirmation:

The universe brings change and challenges to help me grow and evolve.

[Nb: The real power behind affirmations: You have to believe them;
you have to feel them, and you have to live them.]

My Evening Reflections:

What specific actions did I take to proactively shape
my professional and personal life today?

How did these actions make me feel more open to change and
challenges as stepping stones and what did I learn?

Highlights of the day:

Authenticity is the alignment of head, mouth, heart, and feet thinking, saying, feeling, and doing the same thing–consistently. – Lance Secretan

My Morning Prompt

Today, I will embrace being authentic and honour my true self by... *(Write down your thoughts, feelings, and actions).*

I am grateful for... *(Practice daily gratitude)*

Daily Identity Affirmation:

I am true to myself, living authentically in every aspect of life.

Daily Worldview Affirmation:

The universe celebrates my authenticity and rewards my true self.

[Nb: The real power behind affirmations: You have to believe them; you have to feel them, and you have to live them.]

What specific actions did I take to proactively shape
my professional and personal life today?

How did these actions make me feel more authentic
and empowered and what did I learn?

Highlights of the day:

Love is not only something you feel, it is something you do. – David Wilkerson

My Morning Prompt

Today, I will hold space for love in my heart and practice self-compassion by... *(Write down your thoughts, feelings, and actions).*

I am grateful for... *(Practice daily gratitude)*

Daily Identity Affirmation:

I am capable of loving, nurturing meaningful relationships with empathy.

Daily Worldview Affirmation:

In every act of love, the universe conspires to fill my life with joy and connection.

[Nb: The real power behind affirmations: You have to believe them; you have to feel them, and you have to live them.]

My Evening Reflections:

What specific actions did I take to proactively shape
my professional and personal life today?

How did these actions make me practice self-compassion and what did I learn?

Highlights of the day:

Do not follow where the path may lead. Go instead where there
is no path and leave a trail. – Ralph Waldo Emerson

My Morning Prompt

Today, I will look for ways to improve who I am and what I
do by... *(Write down your thoughts, feelings, and actions).*

I am grateful for... *(Practice daily gratitude)*

Daily Identity Affirmation:

I am a creator, turning imaginative ideas into reality.

Daily Worldview Affirmation:

My creativity and innovation are guided by the universe's wisdom.

[Nb: The real power behind affirmations: You have to believe them;
you have to feel them, and you have to live them.]

My Evening Reflections:

What specific actions did I take to proactively shape
my professional and personal life today?

How did these actions relate my effort to improve things and what did I learn?

Highlights of the day:

Yesterday is history, tomorrow is a mystery, today is a gift,
which is why we call it the present. – Bil Keane

My Morning Prompt

Today, I will focus on the present instead of dwelling on the past or being anxious of the future by... *(Write down your thoughts, feelings, and actions).*

I am grateful for... *(Practice daily gratitude)*

Daily Identity Affirmation:

I am mindful, living with awareness and appreciation of the now.

Daily Worldview Affirmation:

In my mindfulness, the universe reveals its beauty and secrets to me.

[Nb: The real power behind affirmations: You have to believe them;
you have to feel them, and you have to live them.]

My Evening Reflections:

What specific actions did I take to be more self-aware
and focus on the present moment today?

How did these actions allow me to create magic in
the present time and what did I learn?

Highlights of the day:

The greatest thing in the world is to know how to
belong to oneself. – Michel de Montaigne

My Morning Prompt

Today, I will practice self-love and self-acceptance, and I will honour
myself by... *(Write down your thoughts, feelings, and actions).*

I am grateful for... *(Practice daily gratitude)*

Daily Identity Affirmation:

I am worthy, acknowledging my inherent value and potential.

Daily Worldview Affirmation:

The universe supports my journey towards self-love and self-acceptance.

[Nb: The real power behind affirmations: You have to believe them;
you have to feel them, and you have to live them.]

What specific actions did I take to proactively shape
my professional and personal life today?

How did these actions allow me to honour and accept
myself for who I am and what did I learn?

Highlights of the day:

Weekly Check-Ins

1. A section to summarise your progress, record any setbacks, and lessons learned during the week.

2. Space for resetting specific goals related to each principle for the upcoming week.

What was the most significant lesson I learned about myself this week?

How have the seven principles guided my behaviour, decisions and actions this week?

What do I want to focus on or improve in the upcoming week?

Notes

Accept responsibility for your life. Know that it is you who will get you where you want to go, no one else. – Les Brown

My Morning Prompt

Today, I will take responsibility for my life and career by...
(Write down your thoughts, feelings, and actions).

I am grateful for... *(Practice daily gratitude)*

Daily Identity Affirmation:

I am in charge of my journey, steering it with purpose and integrity.

Daily Worldview Affirmation:

As I embrace personal responsibility, the universe unfolds new opportunities for me.

[Nb: The real power behind affirmations: You have to believe them; you have to feel them, and you have to live them.]

My Evening Reflections:

What specific actions did I take to proactively shape
my professional and personal life today?

How did these actions make me feel more in control
and empowered and what did I learn?

Highlights of the day:

We delight in the beauty of the butterfly, but rarely admit the changes
it has gone through to achieve that beauty. – Maya Angelou

My Morning Prompt

Today, I will embrace change and take on challenges by...
(Write down your thoughts, feelings, and actions).

I am grateful for... *(Practice daily gratitude)*

Daily Identity Affirmation:

I am resilient, transforming challenges into strengths.

Daily Worldview Affirmation:

Every challenge I face is the universe preparing me for greater things.

[Nb: The real power behind affirmations: You have to believe them;
you have to feel them, and you have to live them.]

My Evening Reflections:

What specific actions did I take to proactively shape
my professional and personal life today?

How did these actions make me feel more open to change and
challenges as stepping stones and what did I learn?

Highlights of the day:

The authentic self is the soul made visible. – Sarah Ban Breathnach

My Morning Prompt

Today, I will embrace being authentic and honour my true self by... *(Write down your thoughts, feelings, and actions).*

I am grateful for... *(Practice daily gratitude)*

Daily Identity Affirmation:

I am genuine, expressing my true self with confidence and clarity.

Daily Worldview Affirmation:

By being authentic, I align myself with the universe's truth and integrity.

[Nb: The real power behind affirmations: You have to believe them; you have to feel them, and you have to live them.]

My Evening Reflections:

What specific actions did I take to proactively shape
my professional and personal life today?

How did these actions make me feel more authentic
and empowered and what did I learn?

Highlights of the day:

We can only learn to love by loving. – Iris Murdoch

My Morning Prompt

Today, I will hold space for love in my heart and practice self-compassion by... *(Write down your thoughts, feelings, and actions).*

I am grateful for... *(Practice daily gratitude)*

Daily Identity Affirmation:

I am cherished and loving, deserving of unconditional love.

Daily Worldview Affirmation:

The universe nurtures my capacity to love and be loved in return.

[Nb: The real power behind affirmations: You have to believe them; you have to feel them, and you have to live them.]

My Evening Reflections:

What specific actions did I take to proactively shape
my professional and personal life today?

How did these actions make me practice self-compassion and what did I learn?

Highlights of the day:

Creativity is thinking up new things. Innovation is doing new things. – Theodore Levitt

My Morning Prompt

Today, I will look for ways to improve who I am and what I do by... *(Write down your thoughts, feelings, and actions).*

I am grateful for... *(Practice daily gratitude)*

Daily Identity Affirmation:

I am a visionary, seeing beyond the ordinary to what could be.

Daily Worldview Affirmation:

In each innovative thought, the universe opens doors of possibilities.

[Nb: The real power behind affirmations: You have to believe them; you have to feel them, and you have to live them.]

What specific actions did I take to proactively shape
my professional and personal life today?

How did these actions relate my effort to improve things and what did I learn?

Highlights of the day:

Time is what we want most, but what we use worst. – William Penn

My Morning Prompt

Today, I will focus on the present instead of dwelling on the past or being anxious of the future by... *(Write down your thoughts, feelings, and actions).*

I am grateful for... *(Practice daily gratitude)*

Daily Identity Affirmation:

I am time-conscious, valuing and making the most of every moment.

Daily Worldview Affirmation:

The universe aligns with my mindful moments, enhancing my clarity and focus.

[Nb: The real power behind affirmations: You have to believe them; you have to feel them, and you have to live them.]

What specific actions did I take to be more self-aware
and focus on the present moment today?

How did these actions allow me to create magic in
the present time and what did I learn?

Highlights of the day:

Love yourself first and everything else falls into line. You really have to love yourself to get anything done in this world. – Lucille Ball

My Morning Prompt

Today, I will practice self-love and self-acceptance, and I will honour myself by... *(Write down your thoughts, feelings, and actions).*

I am grateful for... *(Practice daily gratitude)*

Daily Identity Affirmation:

I am self-honouring, prioritizing my needs and well-being.

Daily Worldview Affirmation:

In honouring my true self, I align with the universe's plan for my highest good.

[Nb: The real power behind affirmations: You have to believe them; you have to feel them, and you have to live them.]

What specific actions did I take to proactively shape
my professional and personal life today?

How did these actions allow me to honour and accept
myself for who I am and what did I learn?

Highlights of the day:

Weekly Check-Ins

1. A section to summarise your progress, record any setbacks, and lessons learned during the week.

2. Space for resetting specific goals related to each principle for the upcoming week.

What was the most significant lesson I learned about myself this week?

How have the seven principles guided my behaviour, decisions and actions this week?

What do I want to focus on or improve in the upcoming week?

Notes

Accountability breeds response-ability. – Stephen Covey

My Morning Prompt

Today, I will take responsibility for my life and career by...
(Write down your thoughts, feelings, and actions).

I am grateful for... *(Practice daily gratitude)*

Daily Identity Affirmation:

I am committed to living a life of responsibility and empowerment.

Daily Worldview Affirmation:

The universe supports my journey of taking charge of my life.

[Nb: The real power behind affirmations: You have to believe them; you have to feel them, and you have to live them.]

My Evening Reflections:

What specific actions did I take to proactively shape
my professional and personal life today?

How did these actions make me feel more in control
and empowered and what did I learn?

Highlights of the day:

Life is a series of natural and spontaneous changes. Don't resist them; that only creates sorrow. Let reality be reality. Let things flow naturally forward in whatever way they like. – Lao Tzu

My Morning Prompt

Today, I will embrace change and take on challenges by...
(Write down your thoughts, feelings, and actions).

I am grateful for... *(Practice daily gratitude)*

Daily Identity Affirmation:

I am open to new experiences, viewing change as a positive force.

Daily Worldview Affirmation:

In every change, the universe is directing me towards new horizons of success.

[Nb: The real power behind affirmations: You have to believe them; you have to feel them, and you have to live them.]

My Evening Reflections:

What specific actions did I take to proactively shape
my professional and personal life today?

How did these actions make me feel more open to change and
challenges as stepping stones and what did I learn?

Highlights of the day:

Always be a first-rate version of yourself, instead of a second-rate version of somebody else. – Judy Garland

My Morning Prompt

Today, I will embrace being authentic and honour my true self by... *(Write down your thoughts, feelings, and actions).*

I am grateful for... *(Practice daily gratitude)*

Daily Identity Affirmation:

I am an original, celebrating my uniqueness in a world of conformity.

Daily Worldview Affirmation:

The universe supports my journey of self-discovery and authentic living.

[Nb: The real power behind affirmations: You have to believe them; you have to feel them, and you have to live them.]

My Evening Reflections:

What specific actions did I take to proactively shape
my professional and personal life today?

How did these actions make me feel more authentic
and empowered and what did I learn?

Highlights of the day:

Love cures people – both the ones who give it and the
ones who receive it. – Karl Menninger

My Morning Prompt

Today, I will hold space for love in my heart and practice self-compassion by... *(Write down your thoughts, feelings, and actions).*

I am grateful for... *(Practice daily gratitude)*

Daily Identity Affirmation:

I am a beacon of love, illuminating the lives of those around me.

Daily Worldview Affirmation:

The universe nurtures my capacity to love and be loved in return.

[Nb: The real power behind affirmations: You have to believe them; you have to feel them, and you have to live them.]

What specific actions did I take to proactively shape
my professional and personal life today?

How did these actions make me practice self-compassion and what did I learn?

Highlights of the day:

Innovation is the ability to see change as an opportunity–not a threat. – Steve Jobs

My Morning Prompt

Today, I will look for ways to improve who I am and what I do by... *(Write down your thoughts, feelings, and actions).*

I am grateful for... *(Practice daily gratitude)*

Daily Identity Affirmation:

I am inventive, finding unique solutions to life's challenges.

Daily Worldview Affirmation:

The universe supports my endeavours to think differently and break new ground.

[Nb: The real power behind affirmations: You have to believe them; you have to feel them, and you have to live them.]

My Evening Reflections:

What specific actions did I take to proactively shape
my professional and personal life today?

How did these actions relate my effort to improve things and what did I learn?

Highlights of the day:

The key is in not spending time, but in investing it. – Stephen R. Covey

My Morning Prompt

Today, I will focus on the present instead of dwelling on the past or being anxious of the future by... *(Write down your thoughts, feelings, and actions).*

I am grateful for... *(Practice daily gratitude)*

Daily Identity Affirmation:

I am reflective, learning from the past while living in the present.

Daily Worldview Affirmation:

Each moment I am present, the universe magnifies the richness of my experiences.

[Nb: The real power behind affirmations: You have to believe them; you have to feel them, and you have to live them.]

My Evening Reflections:

What specific actions did I take to be more self-aware
and focus on the present moment today?

How did these actions allow me to create magic in
the present time and what did I learn?

Highlights of the day:

Never allow yourself to be made a victim. Accept no one's definition
of your life but define yourself. – Harvey Fierstein

My Morning Prompt

Today, I will practice self-love and self-acceptance, and I will honour
myself by... *(Write down your thoughts, feelings, and actions).*

I am grateful for... *(Practice daily gratitude)*

Daily Identity Affirmation:

I am deserving of happiness and success, and I pursue them with passion.

Daily Worldview Affirmation:

The universe conspires to lift me higher as I embrace my worth and potential.

[Nb: The real power behind affirmations: You have to believe them;
you have to feel them, and you have to live them.]

My Evening Reflections:

What specific actions did I take to proactively shape
my professional and personal life today?

How did these actions allow me to honour and accept
myself for who I am and what did I learn?

Highlights of the day:

Weekly Check-Ins

1. A section to summarise your progress, record any setbacks, and lessons learned during the week.
2. Space for resetting specific goals related to each principle for the upcoming week.

What was the most significant lesson I learned about myself this week?

How have the seven principles guided my behaviour,
decisions and actions this week?

What do I want to focus on or improve in the upcoming week?

Notes

The willingness to accept responsibility for one's own life is the source from which self-respect springs. – Joan Didion

My Morning Prompt

Today, I will take responsibility for my life and career by...
(Write down your thoughts, feelings, and actions).

I am grateful for... *(Practice daily gratitude)*

Daily Identity Affirmation:

I am the master of my fate and the captain of my soul.

Daily Worldview Affirmation:

The universe honours my accountability, guiding me towards my highest good.

[Nb: The real power behind affirmations: You have to believe them; you have to feel them, and you have to live them.]

My Evening Reflections:

What specific actions did I take to proactively shape
my professional and personal life today?

How did these actions make me feel more in control
and empowered and what did I learn?

Highlights of the day:

Change is the end result of all true learning. – Leo Buscaglia

My Morning Prompt

Today, I will embrace change and take on challenges by...
(Write down your thoughts, feelings, and actions).

I am grateful for... *(Practice daily gratitude)*

Daily Identity Affirmation:

I am embracing change as the gateway to new beginnings.

Daily Worldview Affirmation:

The universe brings change for my evolution and betterment.

[Nb: The real power behind affirmations: You have to believe them; you have to feel them, and you have to live them.]

My Evening Reflections:

What specific actions did I take to proactively shape
my professional and personal life today?

How did these actions make me feel more open to change and
challenges as stepping stones and what did I learn?

Highlights of the day:

Honesty and transparency make you vulnerable. Be honest and transparent anyway. – Mother Teresa

My Morning Prompt

Today, I will embrace being authentic and honour my true self by... *(Write down your thoughts, feelings, and actions).*

I am grateful for... *(Practice daily gratitude)*

Daily Identity Affirmation:

I am true to my authentic self in all aspects of life.

Daily Worldview Affirmation:

The universe celebrates my authenticity with abundance and joy.

[Nb: The real power behind affirmations: You have to believe them; you have to feel them, and you have to live them.]

What specific actions did I take to proactively shape
my professional and personal life today?

How did these actions make me feel more authentic
and empowered and what did I learn?

Highlights of the day:

The only thing we never get enough of is love; and the only thing we never give enough of is love. – Henry Miller

My Morning Prompt

Today, I will hold space for love in my heart and practice self-compassion by... *(Write down your thoughts, feelings, and actions).*

I am grateful for... *(Practice daily gratitude)*

Daily Identity Affirmation:

I am a source of love, kindness, and compassion.

Daily Worldview Affirmation:

In my expressions of love, the universe brings deeper connections.

[Nb: The real power behind affirmations: You have to believe them; you have to feel them, and you have to live them.]

What specific actions did I take to proactively shape
my professional and personal life today?

How did these actions make me practice self-compassion and what did I learn?

Highlights of the day:

There's a way to do it better – find it. – Thomas Edison

My Morning Prompt

Today, I will look for ways to improve who I am and what I do by... *(Write down your thoughts, feelings, and actions).*

I am grateful for... *(Practice daily gratitude)*

Daily Identity Affirmation:

I am continuously evolving and improving in all areas of life.

Daily Worldview Affirmation:

In my quest for improvement, the universe guides me towards growth and success.

[Nb: The real power behind affirmations: You have to believe them; you have to feel them, and you have to live them.]

My Evening Reflections:

What specific actions did I take to proactively shape
my professional and personal life today?

How did these actions relate my effort to improve things and what did I learn?

Highlights of the day:

*Yesterday is gone. Tomorrow has not yet come. We have
only today. Let us begin. – Mother Teresa*

My Morning Prompt

Today, I will focus on the present instead of dwelling on the past or being
anxious of the future by... *(Write down your thoughts, feelings, and actions).*

I am grateful for... *(Practice daily gratitude)*

Daily Identity Affirmation:

I am living fully in each present moment, cherishing the now.

Daily Worldview Affirmation:

The universe enriches my present moments with joy and purpose.

[Nb: The real power behind affirmations: You have to believe them;
you have to feel them, and you have to live them.]

What specific actions did I take to be more self-aware
and focus on the present moment today?

How did these actions allow me to create magic in
the present time and what did I learn?

Highlights of the day:

The most important day is the day you decide you're good enough for you. It's the day you set yourself free. – Brittany Josephina

My Morning Prompt

Today, I will practice self-love and self-acceptance, and I will honour myself by... *(Write down your thoughts, feelings, and actions).*

I am grateful for... *(Practice daily gratitude)*

Daily Identity Affirmation:

I am living a life that will leave a meaningful legacy.

Daily Worldview Affirmation:

I am open to the universe's guidance and wisdom.

[Nb: The real power behind affirmations: You have to believe them; you have to feel them, and you have to live them.]

My Evening Reflections:

What specific actions did I take to proactively shape
my professional and personal life today?

How did these actions allow me to honour and accept
myself for who I am and what did I learn?

Highlights of the day:

Weekly Check-Ins

1. A section to summarise your progress, record any setbacks, and lessons learned during the week.

2. Space for resetting specific goals related to each principle for the upcoming week.

What was the most significant lesson I learned about myself this week?

How have the seven principles guided my behaviour, decisions and actions this week?

What do I want to focus on or improve in the upcoming week?

Notes

In the end, we are our choices. Build yourself a great story. – Jeff Bezos

My Morning Prompt

Today, I will take responsibility for my life and career by...
(Write down your thoughts, feelings, and actions).

I am grateful for... *(Practice daily gratitude)*

Daily Identity Affirmation:

I am in control of my actions and their impact on my life.

Daily Worldview Affirmation:

The universe supports me as I take charge of my life's narrative.

[Nb: The real power behind affirmations: You have to believe them; you have to feel them, and you have to live them.]

What specific actions did I take to proactively shape
my professional and personal life today?

How did these actions make me feel more in control
and empowered and what did I learn?

Highlights of the day:

He who rejects change is the architect of decay. The only human
institution which rejects progress is the cemetery. – Harold Wilson

My Morning Prompt

Today, I will embrace change and take on challenges by...
(Write down your thoughts, feelings, and actions).

I am grateful for... *(Practice daily gratitude)*

Daily Identity Affirmation:

I am courageous, facing challenges head-on with determination.

Daily Worldview Affirmation:

The universe presents challenges as gifts to strengthen my spirit.

[Nb: The real power behind affirmations: You have to believe them;
you have to feel them, and you have to live them.]

What specific actions did I take to proactively shape
my professional and personal life today?

How did these actions make me feel more open to change and
challenges as stepping stones and what did I learn?

Highlights of the day:

Be yourself; everyone else is already taken. – Oscar Wilde

My Morning Prompt

Today, I will embrace being authentic and honour my true self by... *(Write down your thoughts, feelings, and actions).*

I am grateful for... *(Practice daily gratitude)*

Daily Identity Affirmation:

I am genuine in my actions and thoughts, true to my inner voice.

Daily Worldview Affirmation:

As I honour my true self, the universe reflects back authenticity in my encounters.

[Nb: The real power behind affirmations: You have to believe them; you have to feel them, and you have to live them.]

My Evening Reflections:

What specific actions did I take to proactively shape
my professional and personal life today?

How did these actions make me feel more authentic
and empowered and what did I learn?

Highlights of the day:

I have decided to stick with love. Hate is too great a
burden to bear. – Martin Luther King Jr.

My Morning Prompt

Today, I will hold space for love in my heart and practice self-compassion by... *(Write down your thoughts, feelings, and actions).*

I am grateful for... *(Practice daily gratitude)*

Daily Identity Affirmation:

I am compassionate, understanding and empathizing with others.

Daily Worldview Affirmation:

The universe amplifies the love I give, returning it in abundance.

[Nb: The real power behind affirmations: You have to believe them;
you have to feel them, and you have to live them.]

My Evening Reflections:

What specific actions did I take to proactively shape
my professional and personal life today?

How did these actions make me practice self-compassion and what did I learn?

Highlights of the day:

You can't solve a problem on the same level that it was created. You have to rise above it to the next level. – Albert Einstein

My Morning Prompt

Today, I will look for ways to improve who I am and what I do by... *(Write down your thoughts, feelings, and actions).*

I am grateful for... *(Practice daily gratitude)*

Daily Identity Affirmation:

I am a lifelong learner, always growing and improving myself.

Daily Worldview Affirmation:

As I commit to continuous improvement, the universe guides me towards excellence.

[Nb: The real power behind affirmations: You have to believe them; you have to feel them, and you have to live them.]

My Evening Reflections:

What specific actions did I take to proactively shape
my professional and personal life today?

How did these actions relate my effort to improve things and what did I learn?

Highlights of the day:

The future starts today, not tomorrow. – Pope John Paul II

My Morning Prompt

Today, I will focus on the present instead of dwelling on the past or being anxious of the future by... *(Write down your thoughts, feelings, and actions).*

I am grateful for... *(Practice daily gratitude)*

Daily Identity Affirmation:

I am proactive, seizing the day and creating opportunities.

Daily Worldview Affirmation:

As I value time, the universe unveils its treasures in the now.

[Nb: The real power behind affirmations: You have to believe them; you have to feel them, and you have to live them.]

What specific actions did I take to be more self-aware
and focus on the present moment today?

How did these actions allow me to create magic in
the present time and what did I learn?

Highlights of the day:

It's never too late to be what you might have been. – George Eliot

My Morning Prompt

Today, I will practice self-love and self-acceptance, and I will honour
myself by... *(Write down your thoughts, feelings, and actions).*

I am grateful for... *(Practice daily gratitude)*

Daily Identity Affirmation:

I am embracing every stage of my life with grace and enthusiasm.

Daily Worldview Affirmation:

I am connected to the universe and its infinite possibilities.

[Nb: The real power behind affirmations: You have to believe them;
you have to feel them, and you have to live them.]

What specific actions did I take to proactively shape
my professional and personal life today?

How did these actions allow me to honour and accept
myself for who I am and what did I learn?

Highlights of the day:

Weekly Check-Ins

1. A section to summarise your progress, record any setbacks, and lessons learned during the week.

2. Space for resetting specific goals related to each principle for the upcoming week.

What was the most significant lesson I learned about myself this week?

How have the seven principles guided my behaviour, decisions and actions this week?

What do I want to focus on or improve in the upcoming week?

Notes

In the final analysis, the one quality that all successful people have
is the ability to take on responsibility. – Michael Korda

My Morning Prompt

Today, I will take responsibility for my life and career by...
(Write down your thoughts, feelings, and actions).

I am grateful for... *(Practice daily gratitude)*

Daily Identity Affirmation:

I am the creator of my success through responsible choices.

Daily Worldview Affirmation:

With every responsible action, the universe aligns opportunities in my path.

[Nb: The real power behind affirmations: You have to believe them;
you have to feel them, and you have to live them.]

My Evening Reflections:

What specific actions did I take to proactively shape
my professional and personal life today?

How did these actions make me feel more in control
and empowered and what did I learn?

Highlights of the day:

Challenges are what make life interesting and overcoming them
is what makes life meaningful. – Joshua J. Marine

My Morning Prompt

Today, I will embrace change and take on challenges by...
(Write down your thoughts, feelings, and actions).

I am grateful for... *(Practice daily gratitude)*

Daily Identity Affirmation:

I am courageous, facing challenges head-on with determination.

Daily Worldview Affirmation:

Each challenge I face is the universe sculpting my strength.

[Nb: The real power behind affirmations: You have to believe them;
you have to feel them, and you have to live them.]

What specific actions did I take to proactively shape
my professional and personal life today?

How did these actions make me feel more open to change and
challenges as stepping stones and what did I learn?

Highlights of the day:

Be who you were created to be, and you will set the world on fire. – St. Catherine of Siena

My Morning Prompt

Today, I will embrace being authentic and honour my true
self by... *(Write down your thoughts, feelings, and actions).*

I am grateful for... *(Practice daily gratitude)*

Daily Identity Affirmation:

I am unique and celebrate my individuality.

Daily Worldview Affirmation:

In my authenticity, the universe guides me towards genuine connections.

[Nb: The real power behind affirmations: You have to believe them;
you have to feel them, and you have to live them.]

What specific actions did I take to proactively shape
my professional and personal life today?

How did these actions make me feel more authentic
and empowered and what did I learn?

Highlights of the day:

Kindness in words creates confidence. Kindness in thinking creates profoundness. Kindness in giving creates love. – Lao Tzu

My Morning Prompt

Today, I will hold space for love in my heart and practice self-compassion by... *(Write down your thoughts, feelings, and actions).*

I am grateful for... *(Practice daily gratitude)*

Daily Identity Affirmation:

I am filling my heart with love for myself and others.

Daily Worldview Affirmation:

The universe amplifies the love I share with abundance.

[Nb: The real power behind affirmations: You have to believe them; you have to feel them, and you have to live them.]

My Evening Reflections:

What specific actions did I take to proactively shape
my professional and personal life today?

How did these actions make me practice self-compassion and what did I learn?

Highlights of the day:

The best way to predict the future is to invent it. – Alan Kay

My Morning Prompt

Today, I will look for ways to improve who I am and what I do by... *(Write down your thoughts, feelings, and actions).*

I am grateful for... *(Practice daily gratitude)*

Daily Identity Affirmation:

I am a trailblazer, creating my own path.

Daily Worldview Affirmation:

The universe supports my innovative spirit, bringing fresh ideas and opportunities.

[Nb: The real power behind affirmations: You have to believe them; you have to feel them, and you have to live them.]

My Evening Reflections:

What specific actions did I take to proactively shape
my professional and personal life today?

How did these actions relate my effort to improve things and what did I learn?

Highlights of the day:

To say, 'I don't have time' is like saying, 'I don't want to.' – Lao Tzu

My Morning Prompt

Today, I will focus on the present instead of dwelling on the past or being anxious of the future by... *(Write down your thoughts, feelings, and actions).*

I am grateful for... *(Practice daily gratitude)*

Daily Identity Affirmation:

I am present, fully experiencing and appreciating each moment.

Daily Worldview Affirmation:

The universe aligns with my present focus, enriching my experiences.

[Nb: The real power behind affirmations: You have to believe them; you have to feel them, and you have to live them.]

What specific actions did I take to be more self-aware
and focus on the present moment today?

How did these actions allow me to create magic in
the present time and what did I learn?

Highlights of the day:

Self-care is how you take your power back. – Lalah Delia

My Morning Prompt

Today, I will practice self-love and self-acceptance, and I will honour myself by... *(Write down your thoughts, feelings, and actions).*

I am grateful for... *(Practice daily gratitude)*

Daily Identity Affirmation:

I am nurturing my health and well-being at every age.

Daily Worldview Affirmation:

I am an integral part of the universe, contributing to its harmony and balance.

[Nb: The real power behind affirmations: You have to believe them; you have to feel them, and you have to live them.]

My Evening Reflections:

What specific actions did I take to proactively shape
my professional and personal life today?

How did these actions allow me to honour and accept
myself for who I am and what did I learn?

Highlights of the day:

Weekly Check-Ins

1. A section to summarise your progress, record any setbacks, and lessons learned during the week.
2. Space for resetting specific goals related to each principle for the upcoming week.

What was the most significant lesson I learned about myself this week?

How have the seven principles guided my behaviour, decisions and actions this week?

What do I want to focus on or improve in the upcoming week?

Notes

Accept responsibility for your life. Know that it is you who will
get you where you want to go, no one else. – Les Brown

My Morning Prompt

Today, I will take responsibility for my life and career by...
(Write down your thoughts, feelings, and actions).

I am grateful for... *(Practice daily gratitude)*

Daily Identity Affirmation:

I am committed to taking responsibility for my journey, embracing both triumphs
and challenges.

Daily Worldview Affirmation:

The universe echoes my commitment to personal responsibility, amplifying
my potential.

[Nb: The real power behind affirmations: You have to believe them;
you have to feel them, and you have to live them.]

My Evening Reflections:

What specific actions did I take to proactively shape
my professional and personal life today?

How did these actions make me feel more in control
and empowered and what did I learn?

Highlights of the day:

It is not the strongest or the most intelligent who will survive but those who can best manage change. – Charles Darwin

My Morning Prompt

Today, I will embrace change and take on challenges by...
(Write down your thoughts, feelings, and actions).

I am grateful for... *(Practice daily gratitude)*

Daily Identity Affirmation:

I am a seeker of growth, finding opportunity in every change.

Daily Worldview Affirmation:

In the flux of change, the universe reveals my true potential.

[Nb: The real power behind affirmations: You have to believe them; you have to feel them, and you have to live them.]

My Evening Reflections:

What specific actions did I take to proactively shape
my professional and personal life today?

How did these actions make me feel more open to change and
challenges as stepping stones and what did I learn?

Highlights of the day:

Authenticity is not something we have or don't have. It's a practice,
a conscious choice of how we want to live. – Brené Brown

My Morning Prompt

Today, I will embrace being authentic and honour my true
self by... *(Write down your thoughts, feelings, and actions).*

I am grateful for... *(Practice daily gratitude)*

Daily Identity Affirmation:

I am unapologetically myself, free from the need to conform.

Daily Worldview Affirmation:

The universe honours my commitment to being true to myself, enhancing my
personal journey.

[Nb: The real power behind affirmations: You have to believe them;
you have to feel them, and you have to live them.]

What specific actions did I take to proactively shape
my professional and personal life today?

How did these actions make me feel more authentic
and empowered and what did I learn?

Highlights of the day:

A loving heart is the truest wisdom. – Charles Dickens

My Morning Prompt

Today, I will hold space for love in my heart and practice self-compassion by... *(Write down your thoughts, feelings, and actions).*

I am grateful for... *(Practice daily gratitude)*

Daily Identity Affirmation:

I am grateful, recognizing and appreciating love in all its forms.

Daily Worldview Affirmation:

Through love, the universe shows me the beauty in humanity and life itself.

[Nb: The real power behind affirmations: You have to believe them; you have to feel them, and you have to live them.]

My Evening Reflections:

What specific actions did I take to proactively shape
my professional and personal life today?

How did these actions make me practice self-compassion and what did I learn?

Highlights of the day:

Strive not to be a success, but rather to be of value. – Albert Einstein

My Morning Prompt

Today, I will look for ways to improve who I am and what I do by... *(Write down your thoughts, feelings, and actions).*

I am grateful for... *(Practice daily gratitude)*

Daily Identity Affirmation:

I am setting high standards for myself and achieving them.

Daily Worldview Affirmation:

In my quest for progress, the universe opens paths of advancement and success.

[Nb: The real power behind affirmations: You have to believe them; you have to feel them, and you have to live them.]

My Evening Reflections:

What specific actions did I take to proactively shape
my professional and personal life today?

How did these actions relate my effort to improve things and what did I learn?

Highlights of the day:

Time is the most valuable thing a man can spend. – Theophrastus

My Morning Prompt

Today, I will focus on the present instead of dwelling on the past or being anxious of the future by... *(Write down your thoughts, feelings, and actions).*

I am grateful for... *(Practice daily gratitude)*

Daily Identity Affirmation:

I am mindful, living in the now and savouring life's experiences.

Daily Worldview Affirmation:

In my mindfulness, the universe reveals profound insights and joys.

[Nb: The real power behind affirmations: You have to believe them; you have to feel them, and you have to live them.]

My Evening Reflections:

What specific actions did I take to be more self-aware
and focus on the present moment today?

How did these actions allow me to create magic in
the present time and what did I learn?

Highlights of the day:

I am not what happened to me, I am what I choose to become. – Carl Jung

My Morning Prompt

Today, I will practice self-love and self-acceptance, and I will honour myself by... *(Write down your thoughts, feelings, and actions).*

I am grateful for... *(Practice daily gratitude)*

Daily Identity Affirmation:

I am deserving of happiness and success, and I pursue them with passion.

Daily Worldview Affirmation:

I trust the journey of life, knowing each step unfolds with purpose and meaning.

[Nb: The real power behind affirmations: You have to believe them; you have to feel them, and you have to live them.]

My Evening Reflections:

What specific actions did I take to proactively shape
my professional and personal life today?

How did these actions allow me to honour and accept
myself for who I am and what did I learn?

Highlights of the day:

Weekly Check-Ins

1. A section to summarise your progress, record any setbacks, and lessons learned during the week.

2. Space for resetting specific goals related to each principle for the upcoming week.

What was the most significant lesson I learned about myself this week?

How have the seven principles guided my behaviour,
decisions and actions this week?

What do I want to focus on or improve in the upcoming week?

Notes

Congratulations!
You have completed twelve weeks of the Create Your Reality Journal.

- You made a choice to become a better version of yourself and acted on that choice.

- With clarity on who you want to become and the reality you want to create for yourself, you set an intention.

- You stayed committed to the plan.

- Your consistent practice of the seven principles for cultivating a growth mindset has now put you on a path that's going to unlock your true potential.

- Don't forget, to celebrate your achievements, no matter how small. It is these celebrations that keep you motivated.

Take a few moments to reflect on the habit you have cultivated. I'm sure there may have been times when you got too cozy in bed to write in your journal or too rushed in the morning to spend three minutes preparing your mindset for the day. Well done, for resisting the temptation to cave in to 'I'll do it tomorrow'.

As we come to the close of this short journey within these pages, I want to leave you with a few parting thoughts.

You embarked on this journey possibly seeking change, growth, or even a clearer understanding of your own story. Through each line written, each reflection, and every moment of introspection, you have not just journaled; you have engaged in a conversation with the deepest parts of yourself.

Remember, the person who started this journal is not the same person who concluded it. You have grown, evolved, and transcended in ways both seen and unseen. Each word you penned is a testament to your commitment, resilience, your willingness to embrace change, and your courage to confront and transform your realities.

As you move forward, know that this journal is not an end but a
beacon on your continuous journey of self-discovery and growth.
These principles you have explored and the habits you have cultivated around:

Responsibility

Embracing Change & Challenges

Authenticity

Love – in your heart

Innovation

Time – living in the present

and Honouring You

are now intertwined with your being. They are tools that you can carry forward,
applying them to each new chapter of your life.

You are the creator of your R.E.A.L.I.T.Y., the author of your life's story, and the
architect of your dreams. You may want to continue cultivating this empowering
habit. If you haven't already, let me suggest that you get another copy of the Reality
Journal and stay committed to this path.

Remember, every day is a new page, waiting for your words, your thoughts, and
your unique imprint. Continue to write, continue to grow, and continue to be the
incredible person you are, ever-evolving, ever-aspiring, and ever-inspiring.

When I lay on the floor of my bathroom all those years ago, feeling stuck and
desperate, I knew something had to change. From the depths of despair to where I
stand now, creating self-empowerment programs, and mentoring emerging leaders,
the transformation seems almost surreal. It was the creation of my life manifesto, a
commitment to changing my reality. Taking responsibility, being adaptive to change,
embracing challenges as steppingstones, learning to be authentic and living life
based on my standards, my vision and values, continuously improving, and growing,
living in the present and honouring myself, (the R.E.A.L.I.T.Y principles) that made
all the difference. That moment of putting pen to paper resulted in a realisation that
blossomed into a life-altering journey.

My hope for you, is that you too can harness the power within these pages. May you
find your path, rewrite your story, and discover that you hold the key to transforming
your mindset and therefore your own reality. Your journey of self-discovery and
empowerment starts here, and I am honoured to be a part of it.

Thank you for allowing me to be a part of your journey.

Do tell us how the Create Your Reality Journal has impacted your Life. Email us at info@empoweredbydesign.com.au

Positive reviews from wonderful customers like you will be truly appreciated so we can help others cultivate a mindset of 'I can and I will create a reality of my dreams'.

With warmth and gratitude,

Preetie Boler

References

Rethinking Positive Thinking: Inside the New Science of Motivation by Gabriele Oettingen

The Gratitude Diaries: How a Year Looking on the Bright Side Can Transform Your Life by Janice Kaplan

Writing to Heal: A Guided Journal for Recovering from Trauma & Emotional Upheaval by James W. Pennebaker

Mindset by Dr. Carol Dweck

Becoming Supernatural by Dr Joe Dispenza

Think and Grow Rich by Napoleon Hill

The Power of Now by Eckhart Tolle

Wishes Fulfilled by Dr. Wayne Dyer

Notes

Notes